THE TRAIL OF MY LIFE:

THE GENE ESPY STORY

Gene Espy

Indigo Publishing Group, LLC

Publisher	Henry S. Beers
Associate Publisher	Rick L. Nolte
Associate Publisher	Richard J. Hutto
Executive VP	Robert G. Aldrich
Editor-in-Chief	Joni Woolf
Designer	Scott Baber
Print Studio Manager	Gary G. Pulliam
Print Studio Assistant	Chris Bryant
Front Cover Photo	Gary W. Meek

©2008 Gene Espy

Library of Congress Control Number: 2008939656

ISBN: (13 digit) 978-1-934144-51-0
     (10 digit) 1-934144-51-7

Indigo Publishing Group books are available at quantity discounts with bulk purchase for educational, business, or sales promotional use. For information, please write to: Indigo Publishing Group, LLC, 435 Second Street, Suite 320, Macon, GA 31201, or call 866-311-9578.

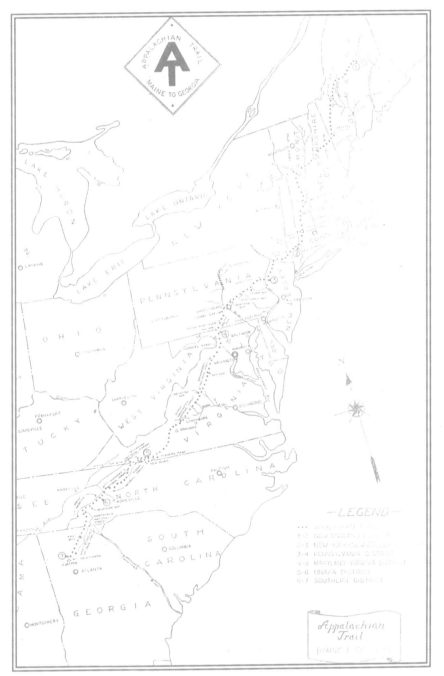

Appalachian Trail, 1951. From the Appalachian Trail Conservancy Archives.

.

DEDICATION

Dedicated to Eugenia Espy, my loving wife for fifty-four years. She gave me inspiration and encouragement to accomplish both my thru-hike of the Appalachian Trail and this book about my adventures.

CONTENTS

Acknowledgments...vii

Foreword..ix

Introduction.. xv

UNIT I

Chapter 1   Exploring God's World.....................................3

Chapter 2   Pranks and Police...15

Chapter 3   Excellent Experience..19

Chapter 4   Seeing the Sights...25

Chapter 5   A Trip by Water...27

Chapter 6   Sharpening Skills...33

Chapter 7   Pranks and Perseverance..................................35

Chapter 8   On Two Wheels and Four.................................43

Chapter 9   Dynamite Adventures......................................49

UNIT II

Chapter 10   Introduction to the Trail...............................53

Chapter 11   Hiking Gear...57

Chapter 12   The Big Hike Begins.....................................63

Chapter 13   Damascus Hospitality....................................79

Chapter 14   Good People and Good Times........................89

Chapter 15   Chance Meeting...97

Chapter 16   Misfortunes of the Soles............................. 101

Chapter 17   Amidst the Cold and the Creatures.............. 107

Chapter 18   Summit Day at Last..................................... 115

Chapter 19   A Royal Reception 119

List of Overnight Stopping Places (1951) 129

UNIT III

Chapter 20   Trail Afterthoughts 137
Chapter 21   Earl Shaffer, My Friend 143
Chapter 22   More Adventures 147

I took pictures throughout my hike with this Kodak 35 mm camera. Photo by Gary W. Meek.

ACKNOWLEDGMENTS

I have been motivated and encouraged by my wife, Eugenia, and our two daughters, Ellen Espy Holliday and Jane Espy Gilsinger to write about my life experiences. Even as they were growing up, Ellen and Jane enjoyed hearing me tell of my adventures, and often told me I should write a book. My granddaughter, Courtney Holliday, enjoys hiking, and has reminded me of some favorite stories to include in the book. Amanda Gilsinger, my younger granddaughter, has been enthusiastic and helpful. She and Courtney want to thru-hike the Appalachian Trail someday.

I am indebted to Kimberly Link-Wills, Managing Editor, Georgia Tech Alumni Association publications for her editing and ideas for the book. Kimberly Link-Wills wrote the prize-winning article about me in the Fall 2005 *Georgia Tech Alumni Magazine*. Also, I appreciate the helpful ideas and editing I received from Anne B. Jones, PhD., a published author.

I am grateful and overjoyed that my friend, Larry Luxenberg, wrote such a fine Foreword for my book. He is the author of the book, *Walking the Appalachian Trail*, the president of the Appalachian Trail Museum, an Appalachian Trail thru-hiker, and a hiker of several other trails. The Appalachian Trail Conservancy staff members, especially Laurie Potteiger, gave me assistance. Thanks to the wonderful Atlanta photographer, Gary W. Meek, who furnished pictures taken at Amicalola Falls State Park, Georgia, of my thru-hike equipment and me for the Fall 2005 *Georgia Tech Alumni Magazine* article.

Larry Caldwell, Washington Memorial Library, assisted with information.

Henry Beers, Publisher of Indigo Custom Publishing, LLC, and his staff provided sound, experienced assistance in this endeavor.

Thanks to all the people responsible for building and maintaining the Appalachian Trail. Hundreds of volunteers in the AT organization spend countless hours working so that every foot of the Trail is kept in pristine condition.

This book could not have been written without my family, my friends, and new friends whom I have mentioned giving me the encouragement and help I needed. My many thanks to all.

I hold half of one of three pairs of hiking shoes I wore out on my thru-hike. Some of my other gear is displayed on the table in this photo taken in 1997 by Woody Marshall for an article written by Ed Grisamore for the *Macon Telegraph* newspaper.

FOREWORD

Over the years, I've interviewed more than 200 thru-hikers and met hundreds, if not thousands, of other long distance hikers. Each has had an unusual story. But for me, one person's stories of the trail have always stood out. Listening to his deep Georgia drawl and his delight in the adventures, I've been enthralled for nearly three decades by the trail stories of Gene Espy.

A barefoot boy from Cordele, Georgia, Gene had a boundless curiosity for the world around him and an endless appetite for adventure. His skills and his adventures built over the years until he became one of the pioneer thru-hikers of the Appalachian Trail and earned a special place in hiking lore.

I knew that as a youth he had some adventures but I never suspected that he had so many widely varied interests and so much energy. He was always in motion, a champion hitchhiker, boat builder, spelunker, motorcyclist and bicyclist. His hitchhiking exploits alone made him a king of the road. Just as "my childhood feet valued their freedom" he was continually on the lookout for new adventures. Once he even captured a small alligator while caving.

While he pulled many pranks and larks and had lots of narrow escapes, Gene also learned the value of careful planning and improvising as he accumulated skills and confidence and came to realize that he could chart his own path. All of these adventures culminated in his 1951 thru-hike of the A.T., only the second time this had been achieved.

Often before one comes to the Appalachian Trail, one is steeped in its mystique. For many years it was the longest continuous marked trail in the world. It is both an opening into the wonders of the natural world and now a social trail, a place where people of diverse backgrounds forge strong bonds and revitalize their lives. But when one sees a stretch of the trail, a few feet wide corridor through the forest, it may seem nothing out of the ordinary. And yet from this blank and sometimes ordinary canvas, extraordinary stories have been formed.

From the first, the idea of the Appalachian Trail seemed so natural that it has always seemed older than it is and exerted a powerful hold on the imagination. What gives the A.T. its special power, the appeal that reaches around the world, is the unique combination of its extraordinary length and natural beauty, its rich history and the special community of volunteer trail builders, trail angels and the moving group of thru-hikers that has become intertwined with it.

This combination is fortuitous but certainly not inevitable. It took special people, people with unusual skill, with determination and the ability to surmount challenges and the creativity to envision their special path. Among these unusual people were Benton MacKaye whose idea it was, Myron Avery, who brought the trail to completion and the early thru-hikers, who provided its mystique, among them Gene Espy, that onetime barefoot boy from Georgia.

Over the first quarter century of thru-hiking, only 33 people completed the entire trail in a single year. In the next three decades, that number has soared and now more than 10,000 hikers are recorded as having completed the A.T. In the early days hikers were so rare that people wondered who the occasional hiker was and some asked Gene why he was hiking "that government trail."

Those early thru-hikers left their special mark, providing a path for their more numerous followers. With that blank canvas, they provided an example, a route, and an inspiration that all later day hikers benefit from. With little to rely on but his prior experiences, ingenuity and wide assortment of skills, Gene made do with what equipment was available, adapted some to his own purposes and willingly endured whatever discomforts couldn't be avoided.

After Gene's thru-hike, he mostly kept his backpack stowed away until March of 1981 when he and three other thru-hikers took a weekend backpacking trip from Mt. Oglethorpe, Georgia, the original southern terminus of the A.T., to Springer Mountain. I first heard Gene tell his trail stories a few months later at a biennial meeting of the Appalachian Trail Conference. Gene invited Earl Shaffer, the first thru-hiker, to discuss their trips in a workshop. Off to the side was Gene's old hiking equipment, perfectly preserved. Gene carefully brought out each piece of equipment, explained the meticulous thinking that lay behind each selection and told the stories that each object prompted. Whether it was a miner's carbide light or an adapted World War II Army surplus steel frame rucksack, each item had its own interest. I was captivated and eagerly sought out other opportunities to hear his stories.

Since then, I've had many chances to listen to Gene and I never tire of his wry sense of humor or enthusiasm for adventure. I've also never exhausted his supply of stories. Many times I've heard of his warm reception in Damascus, Virginia (a great place to spend the night in jail) or of his perilous sleeping perch atop a fire tower. During the night he took refuge on a narrow platform high above the ground after hearing the bloodcurdling screams of some fighting wildcats.

Here are two of my favorite anecdotes. In a time when beards were rare, Gene at 24 years old on his thru-hike soon sported a thick beard. Once someone watching him hiking said, "there goes a spry old man."

Year later, a woman recalled that as he was leaving the post office in Snowden, Virginia, near the James River, he exchanged two nickels for a dime to spare him the extra weight. While Gene doesn't recall the incident, like most thru-hikers, he was acutely weight conscious.

With the 60th anniversary of Gene's pioneering trip coming up, it's easy to overlook how much the thru-hiking experience has changed. Back then, Gene could go for a week without seeing another person and fellow hikers were rare. Gene had to rely on all of his resources and his many skills to safely complete the trail. Little did he anticipate that his boating experience would come in handy on a treacherous passage of the Kennebec River in Maine.

While few people hiked then, there were more isolated farms and ranger stations along the trail route. Gene had many chances to visit the poor but proud mountain people and this greatly enriched his journey. When I think of Gene, I picture an unfailingly polite and spiritual man. One treasured memory is of a Sunday morning sunrise service at the Appalachian South Folklife Center in Pipestem, West Virginia. Gene and Chester Dziengielewski, the third thru-hiker, participated. Gene and Chester, the first person to complete the trail hiking southbound, had briefly met on the trail not far from its midpoint in Pennsylvania and remained friends over the years. As the sun streamed in through the chapel windows and the stories flowed, I could feel the powerful forces of nature and the mysteries of the human condition.

By turns whimsical and serious, confident and determined, Gene describes the youthful adventures of someone the Lewiston, Maine, *Daily Sun* called "a man of fortitude and courage." All who walked in his footsteps owe Gene a debt of thanks for setting such a thoughtful example. He is also a bridge to much of that A.T. history, having known trail founder Benton MacKaye and so many others in the trail community.

Stretching back across time, Gene Espy's memories of his historic 1951 thru-hike remain vivid and fresh and have a timeless quality. I can't remember the last book I've read so fast or enjoyed so much. Now it is your chance, as you turn the pages, to hear the stories yourself and to meet a gentle and caring soul who set out to discover the world and himself and shines a strong carbide light for others to follow.

— Larry Luxenberg

INTRODUCTION

Crunching through dry leaves and looking out at the endless horizon of the Smoky Mountains on a cold February morning as a young Georgia Tech student in 1945, I had no idea I would one day write a book. I did know that a burning desire to hike and enjoy the entire Appalachian Trail kindled in me that auspicious day. Hiking purely as a fun vacation, I indeed reached that goal on September 30, 1951, when I became the second thru-hiker of the Appalachian Trail.

After sharing my memories through the years, I feel an overwhelming need to preserve the history of what I experienced as a pioneer hiker, to record the original conditions and the natural beauty of the Appalachian Trail. I also want to show the ways the Trail journey has changed, to compare early supplies, shelters, and hiking equipment with those of today.

This book primarily highlights that early pilgrimage of 123 days, but other excursions are recorded as well. Looking back, I realize how as a youth, my lack of fear and yearning to explore the world drove me to conquer new things. As each experience unfolded, it increased my courage, my ingenuity, my faith in God, and the confidence I needed to accomplish my goals. A wide variety of demanding activities, such as spelunking, long-distance bicycling, boating, and hitchhiking helped prepare me for the Trail, which was to become the greatest test of spirit and endurance of my life. My desire to hike every foot of the Appalachian Trail has inspired some people to consider me a purist.

For years I have given talks to Boy Scouts, Girl Scouts, schools, civic clubs, church groups, the Georgia Wilderness Society, Amicalola Falls State Park hiker meetings, the Appalachian Trail Conference, and the Appalachian Long Distance Hikers Association. I am often asked if I have written a book of my adventures and experiences.

My adventures happened in a past and sometimes forgotten generation. I enjoy encouraging people to take time from their busy lives and gain some perspective on life by experiencing the natural rhythm of outdoor life as I have.

Standing at Newfound Gap in the Smoky Mountains on June 17, 1951, I am holding my hiking staff in its original length of about four and one half feet. Later, the killing of a striking rattlesnake caused my staff to lose about one foot in length.

UNIT I

CHAPTER 1

Exploring God's World

As a twelve-year-old on a Boy Scout hike near my hometown of Cordele, Georgia, I picked up a long stick in the woods. I wanted to keep the stick but didn't know why. I never dreamed that at age twenty-four, I would be using it to become the second thru-hiker of the Appalachian Trail from Georgia to Maine in 1951, nor could I have imagined the impact that such a feat would have on my life.

When Amicalola Falls State Park put my Appalachian Trail hiking gear on display in its visitors center in 2005, it was a tribute to all of us who have conquered the Trail's rugged paths. Those simple remnants of my journey represent the journeys of many – pilgrimages not only into the physical wilderness but into the depths of our souls.

Although I was unaware of it, I had been preparing for that journey since childhood, determined to conquer every outdoor challenge I could find. The abilities and confidence I gained, together with my intense determination, enabled me to conquer the challenges in fulfilling my ultimate dream. I grew up free to reach as far and high as I could go, always knowing my home base awaited me.

I never saw a mountain until I was sixteen years old. My hometown in south Georgia is best known for the watermelons grown on its surrounding flat farmlands. The place of my birth and my childhood served as the launching pad for my many great adventures and some misadventures.

Both of my parents were hardworking, honest, and individualistic. They met as children growing up in nearby towns in south Alabama.

My father, Lee, served in the United States Army during World War I. Immediately after his Army discharge, he married my mother and brought her back to his Cordele home. He resumed his career as a cotton buyer and later became a bookkeeper at a local hardware store. My father was the more free-spirited parent, so I tended to confide in him more about my exploits.

My mother, Iona Peterman Espy, graduated from Brenau College (now Brenau University) in Gainesville, Georgia, in a time when it was quite unusual for women to go to college. After completing her studies as a music major, she pushed the boundaries further by staying on as a professor of piano and organ. When my father and mother were planning to be married by a justice of the peace in Atlanta, the president of Brenau heard about their plans and insisted they have a nice wedding at the campus auditorium.

She later used her passion for music to organize the Cordele Symphony Club, in which she remained active the rest of her life. Well known in the area for her musical talent, my mother also taught piano lessons in our home.

A proud Southerner, my mother passed down one of her favorite stories to me. When she was a little girl, her uncle, a Civil War veteran from Alabama, would often visit and ask her to play "Dixie" for him on the piano. The first time she was only three years old, but her love for music and her talent were already evident. She loved to play "Dixie" and was thrilled to earn the nickels he gave her in thanks. She saved the nickels for something special, learning early on the importance of following her passion, setting goals, and persevering to reach them.

My older brother, John Lee, born in 1922 as my only sibling, was a big influence on my life. Born in 1927, I aspired as a child to follow in his footsteps. John Lee graduated from Georgia Tech as a chemical engineer. He was more proud of his graduation under the cooperative work/study plan than he was of the "with honor" on his diploma.

He served as an officer in the U.S. Navy during World War II and was stationed at Princeton University for a few weeks. Once when John Lee attended an opera there, the man sitting right in front of him was Albert Einstein.

John Lee went on to get a master's degree at the Massachusetts Institute of Technology and a doctoral degree in business from Harvard University. He explored the world as he later worked in Turkey and was a missionary in Hong Kong.

My brother and I were not among our mother's successful piano students. If we hit a wrong note while practicing, she would hear it no matter where she was in the house, prompting an immediate lesson. She did instill in us a grand appreciation for music that led much later to enjoyment.

During the tough Depression years, Mother combined her strength and endurance with her passion to help feed the family by teaching piano lessons in our home. She also exchanged lessons for art, and those treasured oil paintings hang in our home today.

Our family regularly attended Sunday School and worship services at the First Baptist Church of Cordele, where, after a time of playing for First Methodist, my mother became organist. Even as a toddler, I knew her music was serious business and learned not to disturb her. While she practiced at the church, I entertained myself by rolling marbles back and forth in the slot of the prayer rail.

My brother and I were expected to participate in church every Sunday and remain loyal to our faith. While in primary and junior age Sunday School, I won numerous awards for attendance, sometimes acquiring a much treasured pocket watch. I was active in the Royal Ambassadors, a missionary organization for boys, taking a leadership role as a youngster and later as an adult.

I have continued my involvement and faithfulness, accepting Christ as a teen, and then later marrying a woman whose power of faith matched mine. Both of us have always served in prominent roles in our church.

My wife and I have continued this practice of worship with our family wherever we have lived. At age twenty-seven, I was ordained as a deacon in the First Baptist Church of Cordele. Today in Macon, Georgia, I am a deacon at the Highland Hills Baptist Church. I have enjoyed teaching Sunday School and working with children. Living near the church, I am in charge of the security and have been active in the maintenance over the years. Earl Farriba, my friend and fellow church member, and I have voluntarily worked on plumbing, electrical, air conditioning, and carpentry projects in our spare time. My wife teaches a Bible class for women and chairs the church flower committee.

I have always felt comfortable exploring God's world. Maintaining a close relationship with God certainly sustained me on all of my bicycling, hiking, hitchhiking, and spelunking experiences. I never felt truly alone.

Firmly entrenched in their community, my parents were not the adventurous types, but they gave me the courage to venture outward. I'm said to have been born with a wanderlust, a craving for the outdoors and lands beyond my county's flat horizons. Even today, I yearn to be outside, experiencing the sights, sounds, and smells of nature whether on land or water.

My first mode of transportation was by foot and always without my shoes. The feel of the earth beneath my feet was certainly worth any comments by well-meaning people. Except for dress-up occasions like going to Sunday church activities, as a boy I went barefoot all year round. My school superintendent and teachers knew this and accepted it. One time when it was freezing cold, a new teacher suggested to the principal that something needed to be done in the way of shoes for the barefooted little Espy boy. The principal explained that I had shoes but would not wear them. Little did I know that I was really strengthening my feet for a future hike of more than 2,025 mountainous miles.

As a young child, I was business-oriented and interested in stretching my pocket money. I learned to recognize and capitalize on opportunities. My parents taught my brother and me a good work ethic and the rewards of entrepreneurship.

When I was seven, our downtown A&P and Rogers stores printed their grocery specials on handbills. John Lee rallied his buddies to help him distribute these flyers to homes. Once when he was short of help, he agreed to hire me. When we picked up our papers from Rogers, the store manager refused to let me help, saying at seven years old I was too young. He just did not know what a fine worker I was. For years, when I could, I bought groceries from A&P.

When I was in the third grade, an early morning tornado roared through our neighborhood. I was getting ready for school when the storm blew off our roof and swept away an outside wall. For several months after our house was repaired and we moved back in, much work was still being done on the nearby schools and houses.

Seeing an opportunity before me, I began my first job. I bought Coca-Colas from the local bottler, iced them, and took them around in my little red wagon, selling them to the carpenters and workmen. Each bottle cost approximately three cents and sold for five cents. Since I paid a deposit on the trademark green glass bottles, I waited at each place of sale to get them back. Barefoot as usual, I had to watch where I stepped. Many of the workmen chewed tobacco and the residue was all over the ground and floors.

Desperate to buy a bicycle, I diligently saved my money for years. A month passed before I drank a single Coca-Cola from my supply. Ironically, one of my daughters ended up marrying a man that works in finance for The Coca-Cola Company.

My brother pestered me for days to sell him a bottle of Coca-Cola for three cents. Finally, I accepted his money and handed him one.

As he drank, he complained about how flat it tasted. I stayed quiet, smirking to myself. When he had finished, I gleefully told him he had gotten just what he paid for. His bottle had been filled with the remains I had saved from the previous day's empty bottles. I had drained enough from these to fill his bottle to the right height, put on a cap that looked new, and iced this "special" drink. John Lee failed to see the humor, but it made my day.

In grade school I sold little bags of freshly boiled peanuts that a downtown café owner cooked and sacked up. I received one cent for every five cent bag I sold. Each time I started out with two dozen bags in a flat cardboard tray. The tray was supported by a cord that went around my neck. Especially on Saturdays, downtown pedestrians and store employees were my loyal customers.

Saturday was payday, thus also the big day for shoppers. People were usually paid in cash. In addition to the in-town residents who had the day off, there were hundreds of people from the countryside who came to town. For the most part, they were hardworking, poor farm people, often sharecroppers.

Farm people traveled to town in mule-drawn open wooden wagons and left them tied in a big grassy area on the edge of town while they shopped. Purchases were brought back and left in the wagons while they bought additional items. Things left would always be there when the owners returned.

In Cordele, people shopped at Gleaton's Department Store on the main street and its outlet store in another part of town. While in high school, I worked on Saturdays at the outlet store from 8 a.m. to 11:30 p.m., earning $1.25 for the day. I was a sales clerk, floor sweeper, and stock straightener as well as the delivery and errand boy. After working hard for a year, I was given a raise in pay to $1.50 per day.

The front of the outlet store had a wide sidewalk where I parked my bicycle while I worked. The area was crowded with pedestrians, but they never touched my unlocked bicycle. Crime was a rare occurrence in my small town.

Mr. Gleaton's daughter, Alice Ruth, was a cashier at the store. A classmate and friend, she sometimes would ride with me on my bicycle by sitting on the bar between the handle bars and my seat. I worked hard but always managed to have some fun, too.

For several years the Cordele fans enjoyed the games of the Georgia-Florida Professional Baseball League. My father never missed a local game. Outside the gate he would give me my ten cent admission fee, which I promptly pocketed. A small group of us youth waited outside hoping to get in free by retrieving a foul ball. One time I got in with the very first ball pitched.

When I became older I saw all the games for free by keeping the hand-operated scoreboard located above the center field fence. I operated the lights depicting balls and strikes. After each team batted, I updated the score by hanging a big tin numeral sign.

This experience came in handy when I played for a couple of years on one of three unofficial high school-age baseball teams. Our fields were empty lots with small pieces of abandoned scrap wood for bases. Unlike today's Little League, no adults were involved. Children back then entertained themselves without needing adults or technology.

I spent many hours playing tennis on the two city-owned clay courts just a block from home. One year I represented Cordele High School in singles competition in the annual tennis tournament. Perry Busbee, a student at Vienna High School, beat me. Perry later was my father's physician in Cordele; his brother, George, served as governor of Georgia.

From sixth grade through high school, I played clarinet in the school band, organized and directed by Mr. C.W. Scudder. One time in high school while we were preparing for a big concert, Mr. Scudder had the band practice playing just one loud full note. He intended to surprise everyone during the concert by naming one of us as the

I (left) played in the sixth grade clarinet trio in Cordele, Georgia, in 1938. After continuing through high school, I enjoyed playing in the Georgia Tech Band. Henry Whelchel is in the center and Harry Garwood is on the right.

composer of this one-note piece. Well, at the concert he named me. I proudly stood up and took a bow. My piano-teaching mother in the audience was shocked and quite confused. Later on in high school I earned the Outstanding Band Student of the Year Award.

Mac Hyman was one of my good friends in the band. Later he was the author of *No Time For Sergeants*, a humorous World War II story. The movie version featured Andy Griffith and was a big hit.

As soon as I was old enough, I joined the Boy Scouts and was active in all of its camps and meetings, becoming Cordele's first Eagle Scout. Scoutmaster Palmer Greene was the finest, always patient and encouraging — a model of scouting. Mr. Greene served as the clerk of Superior Court and farmed part time.

When I was working on the bird study merit badge, I would bicycle out to Mr. Greene's farm and use his bird books to try to identify species in his woods and fields. Sometimes when he was driving his tractor, I would meet him at the end of a row and relay names of birds I thought I had observed. He would tirelessly tell me all about these birds and correct any of my wrong identifications. Remembering his teachings later made my Appalachian Trail hike all the more interesting.

Mr. Chase Osborn, the former governor of Michigan, donated eight hundred acres of excellent land near Albany, Georgia, for a Chehaw Council Boy Scout camp. I was one of the staff members for the very first summer session at the Chase Osborn Boy Scout Camp. The council sent out beautiful brochures identifying many fine features of the new camp. When the staff arrived, we only found woods, a creek, a well being drilled, and a mess hall under construction. Apparently, the plans in the brochure were for the future. Despite all of this, we had a fine time at camp. It was a good lesson in being flexible when things are different than you expect.

Sheriff Davis S. Hudson from nearby Worth County was visiting his son, a Scout in the camp, when he was shown a two-foot-long snake

April 12, 1943

Scout Gene Espy
515 14th Ave.E
Cordele, Ga.

Dear Eagle Scout: (Thru Chehaw Council #97)

You have now been granted the rank of Eagle Scout. It is my privilege to congratulate you on behalf of my associates here and the entire National Council. You have worked hard and your standard has been high. Your Scoutmaster, your family and others have helped you, and we are all proud of you.

As you take your place with Eagle Scouts you are in the company of young men who are known to be outstanding in all that Scouting means. People will now expect more of you because of this accomplishment.

The Scout Oath and Scout Law are the principles you have chosen to live by. No matter where you go or what you do these precepts will help you to make the proper choices.

Thousands of your brother Eagles have set aside their Scout uniforms to wear the uniforms of our fighting forces, but they have not set aside the Scout Oath and Law nor have they forgotten the experiences in Scouting; camping, hiking, cooking and the like that have helped prepare them for the job they are now doing.

Never before have Eagle Scouts had greater opportunities than those which challenge today's Eagle Scout. I have the utmost confidence that you will "carry on" in the true spirit of Scouting.

Very sincerely yours,
BOY SCOUTS OF AMERICA

Elbert K. Fretwell
Chief Scout Executive

EKF:vlh

A 1943 letter from the Boy Scouts of America states I earned the rank of Eagle Scout, the first one in Cordele, Georgia.

swimming in the creek near where the Scouts swam. The sheriff got his rifle and ran to the edge of the creek. From about fifteen yards away, he aimed and shot the head off the moving snake! After seeing that, I told friends if I ever wanted to do any crime I would not do it in Worth County. However, I did end up marrying my longtime girlfriend, Eugenia, who was from Worth County.

When I was in high school, soldiers in the National Guard were activated to full-time duty due to World War II. I joined the Signal Corps Division of the Georgia State Guard when it became organized. We proudly wore new uniforms that had been made for the Civilian Conservation Corps, which had just disbanded. The CCC identification patches were replaced with that of the State Guard. With once-a-week and periodic weekend practice maneuvers, I became pretty fast using the Morse code.

Photo by Gary W. Meek.

CHAPTER 2

Pranks and Police

One of my best friends is John Carter, also of Cordele. John and I were in church and school together starting in first grade and continuing all the way through high school. We also double-dated and were in each other's wedding. We have spent many hours sharing our thoughts and to this day remain good friends.

As a boy growing up in simpler times, I did my share of a popular form of entertainment: the practice of playing jokes on each other. One day John and I were boat riding with friends when he asked about my plans for that night. I told him I planned to go bowling on a first date with "Mary," whose family knew John well.

John enjoyed pulling pranks and was good at making up things to do. As a way to spice up my date, he hatched a plot. First John would swap my toy pistol in my glove compartment for his real pistol while my date and I bowled. He then suggested that on the way back to town from bowling we travel on the wilderness-like river road. At a certain spot, he and our other friends would have some brush thrown across the road, where they would stage a fake holdup. The plan sounded good to me.

After bowling, Mary and I drove along the river road, stopping at the holdup site. John came out with his shotgun pointed off to the side away from anyone and shouted, "This is a holdup!"

I reached into the glove compartment and grabbed my gun. It was now a real pistol! I held it out my window, pointed it straight up, and fired. John fell as if I had shot him and fired his gun straight up as he went down. I drove over the brush, and we quickly left the scene.

I never saw the other two friends, although they were supposed to chase us in an old Model A Ford parked nearby.

In planning the holdup we thought my date would surely recognize John and the Model A Ford, but she did not. Mary agreed with me not to tell anyone about what happened. Fearing repercussions from my terrified date, I neglected to tell her the whole thing was just one of our jokes. I drove her home and talked about other things.

Afterward I retraced my route to the river road. My friends had vanished, and I cleaned up the brush left in the road. On the highway going toward home, I was stopped by a speeding Georgia State Patrol car. The trooper asked if I had seen anything unusual on the river road, sharing that he had been told of a gun battle in which one man had been shot. I confessed all about the fake holdup. At the trooper's direction, I led him to the alleged holdup location, where his suspicious, squinting eyes searched all around in vain looking for a body anyway.

I followed him back to Mary's house to await my fate. The trooper met with the family, then told me to contact the sheriff the next day. The next morning I privately told my father of the incident. He was not amused, but thankfully, my mother was never told. I knew the sheriff as a classmate's father. The sheriff nicely explained in our meeting that Mary's family thought I had secured the date with her just to pull that holdup trick. No charges were filed, and all of us apologized to the family. It all soon blew over, but Mary and I never had another date.

Playing with fireworks was another source of entertainment for us, also with its own brand of excitement. When I was in high school, Georgia had no restrictions on fireworks so we indulged in all kinds. We liked the fact that marble-size torpedoes would explode on contact. One time a friend and I were each driving our parents' cars and throwing torpedoes out the driver's window at each other. One of my torpedoes accidentally hit my car's metal window guide and exploded in my face. This really shook me up, but I was not injured. My torpedo-throwing days ended that night.

Firecracker cannons were also popular. One day Bobby Neal and I made several shots from his front steps. We aimed a cannon to shoot its ball at the trunk of a tree across the street. On the next shot the firecracker did not immediately explode. Meanwhile, a police car drove by right in the line of fire. Suddenly the firecracker exploded, propelling the hard ball into the car door just below the policeman's elbow resting on the open window. It took some time to convince him that we had not aimed for him.

One afternoon I had my cannon shooting the ball straight up into the air. At some point, instead of a firecracker, I ignited a much more powerful cherry salute and looked up into the sky to see the ball. After hearing the cannon fire, I never saw the ball. I looked down, and there was nothing at the location of the cannon. The explosion had blown the cannon into smithereens, imbedding the small steel pieces in the wall behind me.

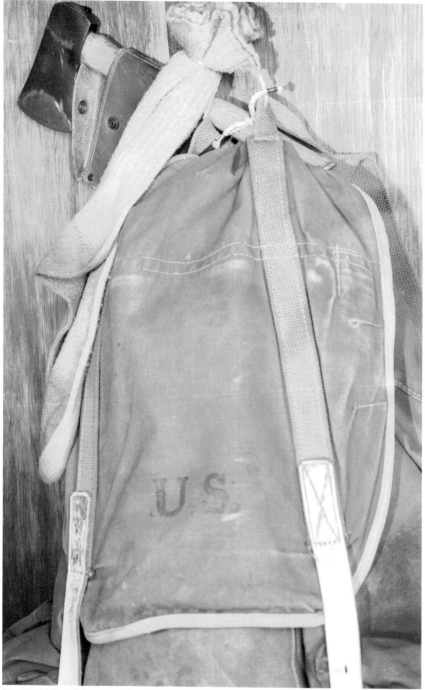

The World War II Army surplus ski troopers steel frame rucksack lasted the entire hike. It only cost $5. Photo by Gary W. Meek.

CHAPTER 3

Excellent Experience

During the summer of 1942, I made my first hitchhiking trip at age fifteen to attend a special Boy Scout training camp at Augusta, Georgia. Even though my parents offered to drive me or pay my bus fare, I welcomed this opportunity for more independence and adventure. And I got it!

Leaving from Cordele I caught rides pretty easily. In Milledgeville I felt lucky when the driver of an eighteen-wheel tank truck offered a ride taking me almost to Augusta.

He had loaded 5,000 gallons of gasoline from a pipeline below Macon to deliver in South Carolina. His truck, typical of trucks back then, did not have the engine power to pull a steep hill as they do now. A person could walk nearly as fast as the truck could go. In going down a hill my driver had to "floorboard" the accelerator to get up speed to ascend the next hill.

We were speeding down one hill at about fifty miles per hour when I heard a sudden explosion. Something dark flew past my window. Our truck was in the left lane headed the wrong direction when we finally stopped. If there had been a car or truck headed our way, there would have been a disastrous head-on collision.

Our truck had blown a tire. Days before this, the nearly worn-out tire had been reinforced with a boot placed inside the tire over the weakened spot. When our tire blew, it was this boot from the tire that flew by. World War II was going on so tires were scarce and rationed. Using flat, rubber-like boots to prolong tire life was common practice during the war.

The truck driver changed the too-hot-to-touch tire, and we continued on. He said he would have no trouble securing a new tire after this blowout. The scary experience did not, however, stop me from riding in trucks with dangerous loads.

Anyway, it was an exciting introduction to the unpredictable world of hitchhiking for me. I got to and from camp safely and had a great time. I was hungry to explore the world more.

At age sixteen I took a 740-mile solo bicycle camping trip from Cordele to the Florida cities of Panama City and Jacksonville and back to Cordele. I had purchased the balloon tire, single-speed bicycle with my Coca-Cola earnings. I rolled all my camping items into my tent and tied this to the steel luggage rack sitting above my back wheel. Eighteen miles into my trip, one of the luggage rack supports broke off at the back axle. I discarded the rack and tied the tent to the top of my handle bar. This was the ideal location as the extra weight was right above the center of gravity of the front wheel.

I could average ten miles per hour and travel about 110 to 120 miles in a day, stopping to eat all my meals in restaurants. At the approach of darkness I would hunt for a school yard, cemetery, or church yard to pitch my tent.

Stopping in Abbeville, Alabama, to visit with some of my father's relatives, I briefly left my bicycle to hitchhike to New Orleans. After seeing the sights there, I caught a ride and at the driver's request drove to Memphis, Tennessee. This was the first time I was asked to drive when I was picked up but not the last. I enjoyed driving the different cars. From Memphis I caught rides back to Abbeville and resumed my bicycle trip to Panama City.

The beach highway along the Florida panhandle was a relatively desolate wilderness. As I was pedaling between towns, darkness overtook me and put my senses on full alert. The waves rolling in crashed even more noisily in never-ending crescendos. The salt air breezes grew stronger. It was just the shadows, water, and me rolling along.

The reflections of moonlight dancing on the water began to play tricks on my eyes. I expected to see a submarine's conning tower rise out of the waves at any minute. This was during World War II. A few months earlier a German submarine had surfaced off the New Jersey coast and let out about twenty would-be saboteurs. I was really scared so I pedaled faster along the deserted beach.

About seventy miles south of Tallahassee my highway ran into Army Camp Gordon Johnston. After stopping me at the entrance, the military policeman gave me the standard thirty-minute automobile pass to proceed. I told him I needed more time to pedal the fourteen miles through the camp. The MP advised me to just keep pedaling and do the best I could. I kept pedaling, but I really took in the sights.

I had not heard of Camp Johnston beforehand but going through it was the highlight of my trip. A World War II amphibious training camp, it provided some of the toughest military training in the world by capitalizing on its sandy beaches, swamps, and jungle-like forests. Combat in the Pacific Islands and amphibious landings and invasions in the European Theater were simulated here. Camp Johnston covered 165,000 acres, including St. George Island and Dog Island, and had about 10,000 soldiers and civilians permanently assigned.

Inside the camp for miles and miles I saw all kinds of interesting amphibious equipment, some with armed guards standing by. On the shoulder of the highway I saw several Army uniform cloth caps, blown off by soldiers riding in open trucks. Metal organization pins were attached to some. I would have loved to have taken some of these as souvenirs, but I was afraid to stop. At the exit the guard just took my pass and motioned me on.

Continuing through Florida, its notorious summer heat rose up from the pavement in steamy waves while the hot sunshine seemed to bake me. Quenching my thirst often became a challenge.

Once I passed a homemade highway sign stating "All The Fresh Orange Juice You Can Drink – Ten Miles – 10 Cents." With more signs tantalizing me as I got closer to the stand, I really worked up a thirst. Finally at the destination was a sign "Closed For The Duration." This referred to the end of the war, whenever that would be, but they did not bother removing all the signs I had seen. Outside the closed-up establishment I operated a water pump by hand a few times, discovering it had to be primed with water before it would work. No such water was available so I had to pedal several more miles to get a drink.

After a couple of more days of pedaling, I arrived in downtown Jacksonville in the late afternoon. I stopped on the sidewalk while a pedestrian was giving me directions to the Callahan highway. Suddenly as a city bus pulled away from the stop, a drunken sailor threw a beer bottle out the window at me, shattering glass all over my foot. Because a bicyclist on the Callahan highway had been killed during the previous week, the pedestrian advised me to use caution. Together with the beer bottle incident, this news had me shook up all the way to Callahan and I gave every vehicle an unusual amount of clearance.

At Callahan a big dog approached me and barked ferociously the whole time I pitched my tent in a schoolyard. I somehow managed to survive intact and fall asleep. I was not feeling good about Callahan until the next day when I enjoyed a big breakfast at the truck stop in the town. When I went to pay, the lady proprietor asked me where I was going and when I would be home. I told her I planned to arrive in Cordele the next night. She refused payment, saying she was glad to help me.

Bicycling on to Georgia I stopped at a farmhouse near the Okefenokee Swamp to ask for some water. When I was invited inside, I saw a pet raccoon running around. What a sight! Raccoons usually do not make good house pets.

I returned to Cordele safely, having made the 740-mile bicycle sightseeing trip in seven days as planned. It was a great trip, even though I had to persevere in the hot summertime. I didn't know it then, but this trip had been excellent experience in many ways for my future hike on the Appalachian Trail.

Closer to home, other adventures awaited me as well. Whether the distance was far or near did not matter, only the thrills of exploring and learning.

When I was a senior, my high school class took a trip to the once popular Radium Springs resort near Albany, Georgia. The resort was built around the huge springs that eventually flow into the nearby Flint River. Here I used my homemade diver's helmet made from a five gallon can that originally contained lard. I had cut two shoulder openings into the sides and padded the can for protection. For vision I installed glass into a narrow opening cut into the can.

To supply air to me, a classmate pushed on an air pump connected to a long hose leading to an automobile tire valve stem mounted on the diver's helmet. Old window weights were tied to the helmet to keep it submerged in the water. In my walk all around inside the springs and their runoff I saw a few fish. After diving I walked along the banks downstream and fished. I quit after I reeled in a twenty-four-inch fish.

This was a good lesson for me in using ingenuity to solve the lack of appropriate equipment. With my engineering talent, I have always enjoyed creating things out of common materials at hand to explore the unknown.

The multi-use Boy Scout knife was helpful to me mainly for opening cans. The film container stored matches used to light my stove and any candles found in shelters. I never built a fire on the entire hike. The gasoline-burning stove was specially adapted by me with an aluminum wire tripod. Photo by Gary W. Meek.

CHAPTER 4

Seeing the Sights

Even with all my outdoor shenanigans, I took my high school education seriously and studied hard. Achieving high scholastic goals was strongly encouraged in my family, so I learned to organize my time well for all pursuits.

In high school I was active in the YMCA-sponsored HiY Club and was elected president my senior year. I was also president of our chapter of the Beta Club, a unit of the National Honor Society. Georgia Tech rewarded me with a scholarship for being the 1944 valedictorian of Cordele High School.

With no senior class trip planned, I left early the morning after graduation on a bicycle trip to Washington, D.C. After pedaling 130 miles, I spent the night in a hotel in Sparta, Georgia. My bathroom was shared with another room. I locked the other door, started the bathtub water, and sat down on my bed. Two hours later, I was awakened by the desk clerk and the traveling salesman I had locked out. They understood when I explained my fatigue from bicycling. Thankfully, the overflow valve had prevented the bath water from running onto the floor.

The next day as I was bicycling on the highway the salesman passed me and stopped. Concerned about me getting sunburned, he gave me some sunscreen to use.

I pedaled to Augusta, where I had to leave my bicycle for repairs. From there I hitchhiked to sightsee in Norfolk, Virginia, and then on to Washington, D.C. I rode the train from there to New York City, where I had a week's reservation at a YMCA. With a city map in hand I walked and rode the subway to various tourist attractions.

In walking through the Chinatown-Bowery section I would step over drunks lying on the sidewalks. I saw a sign "Overnight Room 40 Cents. Guaranteed: An electric light in every room." What the sign did not say was that you would probably have forty-nine roommates. The first ones up the next morning were the best dressed when they left.

I took my first airplane ride to go back to Washington, D.C. Cordele's postmaster, Wiley Johnston, had told me to contact U.S. Representative Stephen Pace, who would be expecting me. To my surprise, when I arrived at his office and told his secretary who I was, she broke into a wide grin and ushered me in to see Rep. Pace with great excitement. It turned out they had expected to see me before I went to New York. Rep. Pace proudly took me to his window and pointed out various sights. Each time I told him I had seen it. Perplexed, with an increasingly furrowed brow, Rep. Pace finally asked me how I had seen all of that. I explained I had bought a Washington, D.C., map and walked all around town. He seemed a bit deflated at this, but was a very gracious host.

My visit to Washington, D.C. complete, I hitchhiked back to Augusta, picked up my bicycle and rode into South Carolina, on to Savannah, and back to Cordele. This was a wonderful trip even though I was disappointed that I could not bicycle all the way to Washington, D.C.

CHAPTER 5

A Trip by Water

Boating and water skiing were other big interests of mine. Showing an early aptitude for designing and problem-solving, I fostered this through creating and making my own boats and skiis.

My parents' home in Cordele had a separate, enclosed two-car garage that I made into a workshop where I enjoyed making wooden boats as a hobby. Made during high school, my first was a simple twelve-foot-long row boat I used for fishing. I even made the oars. I kept it chained to a tree on the edge of Lake Blackshear, ready for me to fish. I often pedaled the ten miles from my house to the boat on my bicycle loaded with the pair of oars, oar locks, rod and reel, 22-caliber rifle, and lunch basket. I delighted in just spending the whole day fishing, enjoying the quiet and solitude. The lack of other people interested in expending as much energy as I did in my exploits never stopped me.

Using purchased plans, I worked on and off for over a year during college on a thirteen-foot inboard, one-step racing boat. It was powered by a souped-up 60-horsepower V-8 engine from a Ford automobile purchased from a classified ad several months before the boat was ready for the engine.

Before installation I took the V-8 engine to Red Vogt, one of the country's best automobile racing mechanics. He operated an Atlanta garage, where he maintained stock car racers for several owners and built racing engines for many other owners. Some of these car owners were "rowdies" whose souped-up cars could outrun any cop on the road. This sport of outrunning the law let drivers hauling moonshine make lots of money. Vogt did a great job of fine-tuning my engine.

This was a powerful engine for such a short boat. The engine had its clutch mechanism so that the engine could idle, but there was not enough room for the transmission to put the boat in the reverse gear needed for docking. Alerted by my father, a manager at the Ford dealership warned that when I launched it and opened the throttle, the boat would have so much power it would try to go straight up.

Several carloads of friends accompanied me for the launching. The boat ran beautifully. It did fifty miles an hour on a half throttle setting. To give the boat even more speed I would need a new propeller with more pitch to the blades. I had so much fun that I never bought the new propeller.

My first long boat trip took place in college with my classmate, Charles Harwell. We used a Snipe he had built – a sixteen-foot sailboat with a high mast, a main sail and a jib sail. We launched in the Ocmulgee River in Georgia and used my nine–horsepower outboard motor for propulsion instead of sailing down the narrow, winding river. It took us nearly a week to reach our destination. We carried a two-man canvas tent and camping equipment.

At night we anchored the boat and pitched the tent using the mast to secure one end of our tent. We slept on the raised floorboards and deck. During the first night we had the daylights scared out of us by a freight train roaring across the railroad trestle where we were tied.

One day as we were refueling our motor, the fast river current swept us under some trees. The mast caught under a limb, causing the boat to tip and dump all of our supplies on deck into the murky water. We frantically grabbed at it all. One thing awash was a large metal container with a hinged lid. For safekeeping I had previously put my expensive new wristwatch in this container that ended upside down in the river. My watch spilled out and my heart sank along with it. Just a few weeks earlier the watch had been a high school graduation present from my parents. I dreaded having to disappoint them with the news when I returned home.

Saturday night we camped out near Lumber City, Georgia. The next morning we walked into the small town and worshipped at a church service.

The Ocmulgee and Oconee rivers came together and formed the Altamaha River. We continued down the Altamaha and docked near a big sunken boat at a huge sawmill at Doctortown. A barefoot night watchman welcomed us for the night. We saw little development along the Ocmulgee and Altamaha rivers.

After a fun day of boating, we docked at Darien, Georgia, on the coast between Brunswick and Savannah, before sailing to Saint Simons Island the following day. When we installed our sailing rudder, there was no place for our outboard motor, so we stored the motor at a service station. The next morning there was little wind, but we did all right sailing anyway.

At that time the bridge from the mainland to Saint Simons was lower than the current one. Our mast was too high for us to sail under the bridge. According to law, sailboats have the right-of-way. As we approached, we blew our mouth whistle. The bridge keeper stopped the cars and opened the bridge for us. The wind died down to nothing and there we sat, idle with no motor or paddle.

It was embarrassing. Cars became backed up from both directions. Irate motorists got out of their cars. Finally, after about thirty minutes the wind picked up and blew us through. Charles's father met us at Saint Simon's with a trailer for the return to Cordele. Dr. Harwell said he, too, was stopped in all that traffic at the bridge. The motorists were so angry he didn't want to tell anyone he knew us. We enjoyed our trip in spite of the bridge incident, which has become more humorous than embarrassing over the years.

In my youth I had been intrigued at the movies as I watched the news reels showing water skiing at Cypress Gardens, Florida, one of the few places where it was done. After high school graduation I ordered a ski-making kit from an ad in *Popular Mechanics* magazine. I bought rope for towing and made a tow handle from a broom handle. I made additional sets of skis from plywood for my friends and me.

From 1947 until 1958 I had a Chris-Craft inboard speedboat and a boathouse on Lake Blackshear, near Cordele. In 1929 the Crisp County Power Commision constructed Lake Blackshear by damming the Flint River. Tree stumps were left in the lake. I cleaned out some of the stumps, often using dynamite, and put out some permanent markers in the lake to make it safe for inboard boating and water skiing.

I was the first to water ski on Lake Blackshear and Lake Allatoona in Georgia. I loved skiing so much that I taught more than a hundred people how to water ski. These experiences on the water gave me confidence and knowledge in handling adverse situations.

Holding the tow rope with one foot, I water skied on the other foot in Lake Blackshear, Georgia. I was the first ever to water ski on Lake Blackshear and Lake Allatoona, beginning in 1947. Performing tricks and sloming became my specialty.

The light- weight L.L. Bean hatchet was used to cut tent stakes. Photo by Gary W. Meek.

CHAPTER 6

Sharpening Skills

Spelunking and my love of exploring the unknown were a natural combination. I had some fun investigating Rock House Cave, a few miles south of Cordele. This relatively small cave was formed too fast to have any stalagmites or stalactites, but it abounds in fossils from various ocean life. To crawl through the main tunnel one has to straddle a small stream. The tunnel leads to a big chamber where the water falls about seven feet and flows off.

On one occasion I was leading a couple of my high school classmates through this tunnel. At the top of the falls, I shined my light around the floor of the chamber. All clear. I handed my light to one of my group and jumped. When I caught my light as it was thrown to me, I shined it in an area of the floor not seen from the top of the falls. I saw an immobile two-and-a-half-foot alligator. Evidently the alligator had been washed into the chamber.

As the other boys jumped down, I was looking for but did not see any more alligators. As I had seen in the movies, I fell forward with my hands on the snout and tail of the alligator. It quickly came to life. We laid a small diameter piece of drift log beside him and tied him to the log, then carried him out. He enthralled the students at our high school before we untied and released him at the Flint River.

While in college, I explored much larger caves in North Georgia near Rome, Kingston, and Cartersville. As far as I knew, these caves and Rock House Cave were on private land but spelunkers were welcome. You didn't ask anybody – you just went in. In many of the caves one would see several strands of string that previous explorers had let out to guide them back out of the caves. It is easy to get lost in some of the bigger caves, but I never used string as I could always remember the way I entered.

One time a fellow spelunker and I were walking inside a cave. We stopped and were standing there talking. He suddenly disappeared from sight. The cave floor had collapsed, causing him to fall about six feet. He was unhurt, and I pulled him from the hole. We kept on exploring new areas.

In the most remote part of each of these North Georgia caves I found the letters ACK burned into the wall. These belonged to an ardent spelunker, Earnest Ackerly, whom I later met and introduced to Rock House Cave. It was always fun to share my interests.

My spelunking experiences sharpened several skills, including my sense of direction and ability to remain calm in unexpected situations. Later, while hiking on the Appalachian Trail, this knowledge was helpful in keeping up with where I had hiked and finding the Trail in unmarked areas, as well as preventing panic when hiking in the dark.

CHAPTER 7

Pranks and Perseverance

In the fall of 1944 I enrolled at Georgia Tech and was assigned to Knowles Dormitory. U.S. Navy and Marine V-12 program students utilized all the other dormitories. As an incoming freshman I anticipated a lot of extracurricular activities in addition to the intense academics. According to strict tradition, freshman in 1944 wore Georgia Tech gold cloth "RAT caps" to designate our status at all school activities. It spotlighted us as targets with a capital T.

As customary at the beginning of fall semester, some of the upperclassmen would haze the freshmen – usually just after dark. One night I was on the roof, ready for them with a huge trash can filled with water. Just as five of them started to enter the dorm I let loose the water, soaking two of them. I ran and hid behind a chimney on another part of the roof. Fearing the inevitable repercussion in the face of stacked odds, my heart was beating wildly. I was breathing so hard I thought for sure people all over the campus could hear me. To my great surprise, the upperclassmen did not even consider the water could have come from the roof. I was not pursued, and no one ever knew I was on the roof with the water.

The flagpole on campus was not safe from mischief either, even though the V-12 military students raised and lowered the American flag on campus each day with the proper ceremonies. One Halloween night pranksters hoisted a wooden outhouse up the flagpole in such a way that it could not be lowered. After a few days the Georgia Tech Y Cabinet (YMCA), for which I was vice president, did a service project of calling the fire department to remove the outhouse and restore the hoisting cords.

Always on the lookout for adventure, my fellow freshman Charles Harwell and I walked by the towering freestanding chimney on campus one Saturday afternoon. Built in 1915 for the heating and cooling plant, it is called "The Stack" and stands 206.5 feet tall. The top was girded with scaffold boards for repairs in progress. A cable running from top to bottom along the brick chimney held sections of wooden ladders.

We felt challenged to climb the ladders to the top. Going first, I climbed hand over hand for what seemed like forever. I reached the top and sat on the open scaffold, realizing then that Charles had ceased to take part in any recent conversations with me. I looked down and saw Charles standing on the ground with several other students. The view from the top at 23 stories high was exciting. I was the tallest thing around! The Biltmore Hotel, blocks away, could readily be seen.

When I climbed down after a few minutes, the campus policeman was waiting for me. I nervously smoothed things over and no action was taken. Later Charles told me that the policeman had walked up and remarked to the group about how high that workman was. The policeman was astonished when someone told him that the climber was not a worker but a student.

Stone Mountain near Atlanta was another good place for me to explore while in college. At 1,686 feet high, it is the largest exposed granite mass in North America. Three figures depicting leaders of the Confederate States of America – Stonewall Jackson, Robert E. Lee and Jefferson Davis – are carved on one side. The sculptures were started in 1923, but they were completed in 1972.

When I was at Georgia Tech, Stone Mountain was a quiet undeveloped area with no commercialization. The as yet unfinished carvings were on the steep side. Energetic walkers could ascend using the sloping side. It was popular for hayrides from all around Atlanta to travel to the base of the sloping side of the mountain.

One afternoon Charles and I walked to the top and descended partly down the steep side to just above the carved figures. Ignoring the obvious danger, I ended up going the last perilous part alone. Observing that several cars had actually pulled off the highway below to watch me in yet another daring feat, I got scared as the reality sunk in. I gingerly crawled on all fours back up the mountain to safety after seeing the unfinished carved figures up close.

I made the most of my college years, including playing the clarinet in the Georgia Tech Marching Band and its subsets, the Concert Band and the ROTC Band. The director, Mr. A.J. Garing, had played in the famous John Phillip Sousa's band. I was thrilled with all the Sousa marches that he taught us to play, and they remain among my most favorite pieces of music today.

When I played as a freshman, nearly all the band members were V-12 military students. One day the Army ROTC Band had a big exercise with the Army ROTC infantry at the Rose Bowl field at Georgia Tech. Infantry personnel stood in their units to watch the band march and play across the field in front of them.

The next march to be played was passed along row by row, originating with the drum major. I was midway in the formation, thinking this was an opportune time to have a little fun with the irritating drum major. When the announcement reached me, I changed the chosen piece. The drum major raised his baton, the snare drums rolled off, and the front and back halves of the band played a different piece. Although I laughed to myself, how it happened remained a mystery to everyone else. Only in recent years have I revealed this mischievous caper.

I roomed in the Georgia Tech YMCA, now the Georgia Tech Alumni House, on the third floor, occupied entirely by students. One free telephone in the hall served everyone. The rooms were set up in suites with two rooms and a connecting bath. One of my suite mates, participating in the co-op program, worked on the other side of Atlanta. He detested having to change city buses to reach his job. I sold him my well-worn but trusty bicycle for twenty dollars so he could ride it to work, saving money and time.

One afternoon I walked by the restaurant next to the YMCA and saw his unlocked bicycle outside. I saw him eating supper inside the restaurant, but he did not see me. Prank time! I swiftly rolled his bicycle next door and left it. I went up to his third floor room and lowered my cave-exploring rope from his window. A friend tied the bicycle onto the rope and I hoisted it, securing it just outside the window. My suite mate came out and frantically searched in vain for his bicycle.

About an hour later he received a call from someone claiming to be with the Atlanta police. The caller said the police had picked up a stolen bicycle and my suite mate could come to the police headquarters, identify and pick it up. When my suitemate went to the nearby bus stop, I rushed out and showed him his hanging bicycle visible from the bus stop. Since he was a little upset, it took a couple of days to get my rope back. My suite mate did forgive me, and we remained friends, and returned to more serious endeavors.

* * *

During World War II, all U.S. males registered for the draft at age eighteen. At age seventeen, I passed a Captain Eddy test that qualified me to join the Navy as a Seaman First Class and receive special training in radar and electronics. When I was sworn in, the Navy ordered me to complete my spring semester at Georgia Tech. Upon completion I contacted the Navy and went home to await orders to report for active duty.

After a few days of waiting, I grew restless, so I took another solo bicycle trip to Florida. This time I pedaled to Silver Springs and Daytona Beach, then back to Cordele. When I passed through

Callahan, Florida, I planned to have lunch with the woman who had given me a free meal two years before. I found her restaurant closed. Perhaps she gave away too many free meals.

Two days after arriving back home, the Navy called and ordered me to report for active duty the next morning. As a Seaman First Class I was in charge of a small group of inductees traveling by train from Atlanta to the Great Lakes Navy Training Center near Chicago. This was my first and only ride in a Pullman car, and it was great!

Due to my bicycle trip, the physical training during the first five weeks of boot camp was a snap. Then came work week with all kinds of K.P. and cleaning assignments. My group was scattered around on various jobs that I didn't relish doing. I soon learned that you were given more work if you were caught standing around. The secret to less work was to disappear!

I saw a way to both disappear and explore. For several days I climbed inside a thirty-six-inch diameter concrete storm water drainage pipe and crawled underground all over that part of the base. I carried a short board to make a seat to rest above the water inside the pipe. Sometimes I carefully lifted steel manhole covers to see where I was. One time I did this only to discover I was under the highway outside the main base entrance. I saw two Shore Patrol personnel, but I eased the manhole cover down before they saw me.

During my boot camp training, I spent several weekend passes in nearby Chicago or Milwaukee. The city buses were free to all military personnel. The United Service Organization (USO) places were always great, giving free food, prime theater and stage event tickets, and various other services. The city people would bring homemade cakes, pies, and other food to the USO locations.

Boot camp was fun, but at the end I told the Navy I wanted to use my week of leave time to go to Georgia. Using money from my pay, they gave me a round-trip train ticket to Cordele. They said there would be no refunds. To see if I could get there quicker, I put this ticket in my pocket and hitchhiked to Cordele and back to Chicago. During World War II, uniformed military easily caught rides. I beat the train time both ways. Later I found out they did give refunds, so I got my money back.

After my discharge from the Navy, I returned to Georgia Tech where the G.I. Bill gave me free tuition and $65 per month. For transportation, I bought a used Servi-Cycle. A cross between a motorized bicycle and a motorcycle, this two-wheeler averaged thirty miles per hour on the highway. Each of the 150-mile trips between Atlanta and Cordele took five hours. It was an uneasy feeling sometimes when cars or trucks would have to follow me for several miles before they could pass me.

One Sunday night on a trip returning from Rome, Georgia, I had motor trouble in the rain. I stopped next to a traffic light to repair my Servi-Cycle without a flashlight. Each time the traffic light turned caution yellow, I could see a bit to work. A kind motorist stopped for me to work under his headlights. Finally, at his suggestion I hid my vehicle in the nearby woods and accepted a ride with him back to my dorm. I went back the next day and successfully repaired my Servi-Cycle.

* * *

During college summers I delivered mail in Cordele covering a bicycle route. On my first day the assistant postmaster showed me my route, which crossed the busy highway to Florida that tourists used. He never mentioned the U.S. mail collection box on this highway that was between my route and another. I had never been directed to collect mail from it.

After a week of delivering I had some curiosity about the box so I opened it. To my surprise it was packed full! I'll bet some of the Northern tourists passing through town wondered why their picture postcards took so long to get to their friends and relatives back home.

I always collected from the mailbox after that. The assistant postmaster never heard about the delay.

For a couple of weeks during the holidays, I used my bicycle to deliver special delivery mail, mostly Christmas cards and letters, for a few cents each. I noticed the majority of these had been mailed at Detroit, Michigan, or Jacksonville, Florida.

Since I was a stranger and not in a postman's uniform, nearby neighbors of the addressee sometimes hesitated to assist me, thinking I was a bill collector. Looking out for the addressee, they replied to me that so-and-so was nowhere around. After I showed them I had a special delivery letter, they would say, "Oh, Mr. So-and-So? He lives right here!"

During the school year at Georgia Tech, I had a part-time job with the Presbyterian literature office in the Henry Grady Hotel building in downtown Atlanta. I would periodically stop by and prepare the church literature orders for mailing. In the absence of a postal meter, I applied the postage stamps. I found out they liked me because I did not steal their stamps.

Additionally, I did yard work at several wealthy residences in Atlanta and I worked part time at the Georgia Tech YMCA customer service counter. Every Friday night I operated the projector to show free Hollywood movies. The projectionist had to change reels several times during the movie. One night I made a change, the movie continued, and a few minutes later I heard the noise of loose film. I discovered the film had not been properly inserted in the take-up reel and had spilled out all over the dark projection room. What a mess! The audience patiently waited while I rewound the voluminous tangles of film.

The Georgia Tech YMCA bought a 1.5-ton Dodge truck for campus groups to use mainly for hay rides. As I was one of the authorized drivers, I received payment and also enjoyed bringing a date along.

I have always cherished these work experiences. They taught me discipline, self-motivation, perseverance, and ingenuity. My thru-hike later on the Appalachian Trail certainly necessitated all of these.

CHAPTER 8

On Two Wheels and Four

I certainly had car adventures as well. My first car, bought during my college years, was a black 1931 Ford that I kept only a few months before I sold it. Later I paid forty dollars for a beat-up but running 1937 Ford with a V-8 60-horsepower engine. Having been used on unpaved roads, it was saturated with red clay dust. The tires were nearly worn out, and I had no spare.

In my workshop at my parents' home during the 1949 summer break, I removed all the seats and wiring and tore out all the inside upholstery and ceiling fabric. While waiting for the complete set of wiring the Ford distributor had ordered for me, I used my parents' car to date my future wife, Eugenia. I had met her through a mutual friend several months earlier. She lived eighteen miles out in the country, and telephones were not available in her area.

The telephone company in her area was privately owned by a local family who required each family to coordinate and pay for installing the telephone poles on their own before the company would run the wiring. Due to limitations during World War II it was virtually impossible for rural families to provide this for the several miles each required for phone service. Consequently, most families in her area did not receive phone service until the mid-1950s.

One morning at breakfast my parents reminded me of their plans to use their car that night. I had no way to get in touch with Eugenia to call off our date for that evening so I went as usual to Plan B. I would just have to use my old stripped-out car. As soon as I got home from my bicycle mail route, I hurriedly began to ready this old 1937 car by running wires to the lights and hot wiring the engine. More than an hour late, I sat on a small wooden box to drive to Eugenia's. I had reinstalled the rear seat so she could sit back there as I drove. My bicycle along with a flashlight and set of tools lay on the bare floor.

Gassing up at an all-night service station where I regularly traded, the attendants had a big laugh when they looked inside my car. I took off and sped to see Eugenia. A rear tire blew, but I kept going. The car rocked from side to side, adding to the comical scene. Just before my arrival, I got out to change clothes and smelled gasoline. The blown tire had knocked loose the filler pipe to the gas tank. I drove on to her home spilling gas the rest of the way. Eugenia was waiting for me as she knew I would never "stand her up." I only stayed an hour due to my car situation. We had fun laughing about it.

When I left her, I rode my bicycle to Cordele, grateful for my preplanning. One of the gas station attendants who had seen me leave laughed heartily at the sight of me on the bicycle.

I successfully repaired and used my car, except for a couple of mishaps, when I was back at Georgia Tech. Driving through downtown Atlanta on busy Peachtree Street on my way to spend Christmas in Cordele, my car stalled. A courteous truck driver pushed me off, but my transmission locked up.

For five dollars, a wrecker service towed my car to the edge of a Georgia Tech parking lot, carefully positioning the engine under a big tree limb. After the Christmas break a classmate took me back to Georgia Tech with a chain hoist and a good used transmission I brought from home. I hooked the hoist to the tree, pulled the engine, and swapped the transmissions. I was truly a "shade tree mechanic" on that one. I enjoyed the challenge of fixing things and saving money at the same time.

Another car problem developed when John and I planned to drive the 1937 Ford from Atlanta to the Mardi Gras celebration in New Orleans. We left Atlanta on Sunday night before the big parade on

Tuesday. We were speeding along on the highway close to Newnan, Georgia, when the engine slung a piston rod. One piece of the rod knocked a small hole in the oil pan. The piston for that cylinder was deactivated and out of the way. Running on the seven remaining cylinders, the car made a knocking sound and motor oil continually leaked out through the hole in the oil pan.

We drove to an all-night service station and were permitted to raise my car on the grease rack to assess the damage. I had the tools, but the attendant did not allow any work for fear of tying up his grease rack. Instead he gave us several gallons of used oil. Periodically we stopped and poured in oil to replenish that which had leaked out.

When the Newnan Ford dealership opened, we drove the car in for an estimate to repair the engine. They could not fix it for the fifty dollars we had to spend but gave us more used oil for our trip back to Atlanta.

We returned to Atlanta, ending the trip for John. Nevertheless, I was determined to go. I bought a one-way airplane ticket to New Orleans. On Monday night before we landed, my seatmate, a New Orleans native, strongly advised me that all the hotels were filled and I needed to look elsewhere. I thought I would try it anyway as I don't give up easily.

I went to a downtown New Orleans YMCA where visitors were being turned away. At the front desk I presented a Georgia Tech YMCA letterhead that listed me as the student vice president. The manager offered two nights in the room used as their infirmary for two dollars a night. I agreed, and as it happened, the infirmary was not used during my stay.

I had a big time! I climbed up a pole in front of the St. Charles hotel and got a Mardi Gras flag for a souvenir. Toward the end of the parade a float based on the popular song "Frankie and Johnny" came by the crowded sidewalk where I was. Johnny removed his hat and sailed it into the crowd. I reached up and caught it.

When I started hitchhiking back to Atlanta, a car carrying two couples sped by me. I knew couples rarely picked up hitchhikers. But, one of the numerals on their front license plate indicated Birmingham, and Birmingham was on my way. I yelled "BIRMINGHAM!" The car stopped, and I ran to get in.

The people asked me in what part of Birmingham I lived. I sheepishly explained how I had just wanted them to stop for me. Things got off to an awkward start but soon picked up. In fact, they went out of their way to show me some points of interest in Birmingham and to take me across town to the Atlanta highway. I soon caught a ride to Atlanta.

Once again the '37 Ford was repaired and I kept it several years. When I graduated from Georgia Tech, my parents generously gave me a new Chevrolet as a gift.

But before that I had a World War II Army Harley-Davidson 45 motorcycle I bought from a graduating Georgia Tech senior. Starting the motorcycle required jumping on the kick starter. A few days after I bought it, I rode it to the Great Smoky Mountains for a weekend of camping and hiking.

About sundown Sunday I was in Gainesville on the two-lane highway to Atlanta. I followed a gray car for several miles before seizing the opportunity to pass it. When I got alongside the car, it suddenly turned left into my path. I put on brakes and hit the left shoulder of the road. I was not injured, but when I stopped, my motorcycle was headed back the way I had come. The driver of the car was taking his family to a little country church. He never saw me. My thought was, "I should be going to church, too!"

One night a few months later I was on my motorcycle heading for a date across town in Atlanta. Near her neighborhood I made a left turn on a through street. A motorist had stopped with his headlights toward me, somewhat blinding me. I did not see the red clay on the pavement and as I turned, my motorcycle skidded on its side. I "mopped up" the clay as I went round and round. I got up and drove on to see my date. When I arrived, she held her garden hose for me to wash the red clay off the side of my good suit.

Other adventures include the time I rode my motorcycle to the top of Stone Mountain near Atlanta. That took some effort!

Since my parents were never told that I had the motorcycle, I could not ride it home to Cordele. When I needed to go home, I would stop in Vienna, leave it at a service station, and hitchhike the ten miles into Cordele. On my return, I would hitchhike into Vienna and then ride my motorcycle back to Tech. The reason I wouldn't tell my parents was that they were still mourning the loss of my cousin. An only child, he had recently been killed in a motorcycle accident the day after he graduated from Auburn University in Alabama.

After graduation I sold the motorcycle for $150 – exactly the same amount as I paid for it. Recently a local motorcycle dealer told me that today the same Harley-Davison would bring $100,000!

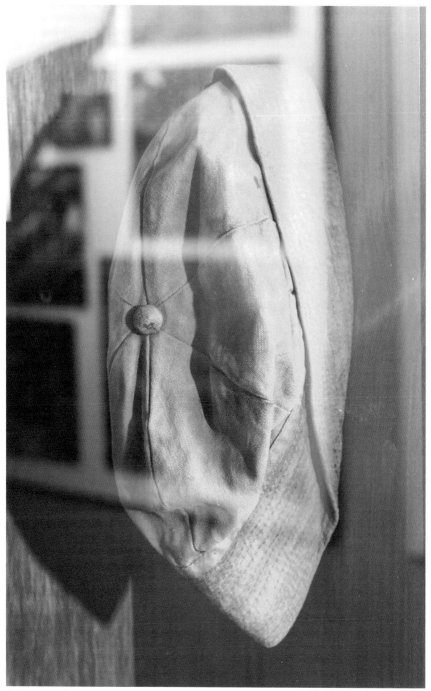

I placed each day's guide information and maps under my Jones type hat. This made it convenient to refer to this info. Photo by Gary W. Meek.

CHAPTER 9

Dynamite Adventures

Thinking I would enrich my college experience, I joined a fraternity but soon discovered that I didn't care for its popular pastime of heavy drinking. I preferred to hitchhike on weekends for fun.

As I was hitchhiking one day, a University of Georgia alumnus headed for Macon, Georgia, picked me up in Atlanta. I put my coat on top of his coat on the front seat between us. When he stopped to let me out at Barnesville, I grabbed my coat and he drove off. A few minutes later as I put on my coat I discovered I had accidentally also picked up his coat. He was already on his way to Macon.

A University of Georgia Bulldog giving a ride to a Georgia Tech Ramblin' Wreck and the Tech boy stealing his coat — this would never do! I ran back to the Macon highway to try to catch a fast ride and overtake the driver.

After fifteen minutes of anxious waiting I caught a ride to Macon. We overtook the Georgia alumnus on the outskirts of Macon. He had not missed his coat, but he sure was grateful for my heroic effort in returning it. I was able to continue hitchhiking on to Cordele from Macon.

Once I told some of my Georgia Tech classmates that the following weekend I planned to hitchhike from Atlanta to St. Louis and return the same weekend. They did not think it was possible, even for me.

After classes Friday afternoon I started my trip, dressed as usual with nice clothes and neck tie. A big Georgia Tech decal was on my overnight bag. My first ride ended at Cartersville, Georgia, then I caught a ride straight through to Indianapolis. This was out of the way to St. Louis, but I didn't mind because I was just sightseeing.

"Danger – High Explosives" was written all over one eighteen-wheeler truck that later stopped for me. As I got in I asked the driver what kind of load he had. "Dynamite!" he exclaimed. He then revealed he was not supposed to have anyone riding with him but he was sleepy and needed somebody to talk to. Needless to say, I kept up a good conversation during the sixty miles I accompanied him.

About 10:30 a.m. Saturday I was in St. Louis, having made excellent time. I didn't know anyone in St. Louis, but it seemed to be an interesting city. As proof of reaching St. Louis as planned, I mailed a postcard to one of my classmates. Then I headed for the highway to Little Rock, Arkansas. By midnight Saturday I was in Blytheville, Arkansas. The traffic had about died out and since I had had no sleep the night before, I looked for a place to spend the night. A "closed for the weekend" service station had a big show window with about an eighteen-inch-wide bottom ledge. I pulled a blanket out of my bag and slept on the ledge, keeping the Georgia Tech logo displayed. No problems.

Early Sunday morning I caught a ride to Memphis. From there I rode with two company executives driving to Atlanta. They set me up to a big Sunday lunch in Alabama and then drove me right to Georgia Tech. At 5:30 p.m. Sunday, I arrived back in my dormitory. Needless to say, my classmates were shocked as they did not think it could be done. From Friday afternoon to Sunday afternoon I had traveled sixteen hundred miles through eleven states and had spent $2.35. Of my many hitchhiking trips this was the best.

UNIT II

CHAPTER 10

Introduction to the Trail

I first heard about the Appalachian Trail in 1939 when my seventh grade teacher, Mrs. Evelyn Fleming, told my class about it. That its southern terminus is in Georgia intrigued me. I became quite interested in it, even though I had never seen a mountain at the time.

Benton MacKaye, of Shirley Center, Massachusetts, published the idea for the Appalachian Trail in 1921 in the *Journal of the American Institute of Architects*. As a forester, author, and philosopher, he was interested in the Trail's role in promoting wilderness as a recreation source. It would serve as a "backbone" linking wilderness areas for people in the cities along the Atlantic seaboard.

It was another man, Myron Avery, who brought the MacKaye dream to fruition. He was more interested in connecting the sections of the trail in a continuous path stretching from Maine to Georgia. One of the most prominent Appalachian Trail workers, Avery personally led the big effort to physically locate, identify, measure, mark, and describe the Trail. The first to hike the entire Appalachian Trail in segments over a period of time, Avery also served as the chairman of the Appalachian Trail Conference (ATC) for many years until his death in 1952.

The entire Trail was completed in 1937, but little hiking or maintenance was done during the following years. With the entry of the United States into World War II, much of the activity in connection with the Appalachian Trail ceased. Many of the Trail enthusiasts were serving in the armed forces or working in the war effort.

My Boy Scout activities kept alive the thought of having adventures in the great outdoors. All the hiking and camping experiences combined to give me an excellent foundation for further expeditions such as hiking in the mountains.

The Appalachian Trail caught my attention again in February 1945, when a Georgia Tech classmate invited me to spend a semester break camping and hiking the Appalachian Trail and some side trails. With our backpacks we hitchhiked to the Great Smoky Mountains and began my first mountain adventure. The brochure we were using as a guide showed a trail shelter on the Appalachian Trail at Spence Field. We searched a long time, even hiking up neighboring Mount Thunderhead, but could not find this shelter the first night. It was midnight when we hiked back to Spence Field still looking for the shelter. We gave up, and instead of pitching our tent, we bedded down on the tent flattened on the ground.

A short time later a sudden rainstorm soaked us. At daylight I put my six soaked blankets in my pack and we started hiking. It was a beautiful sunny day but I did not think to stop and dry my blankets. That night at the Silers Bald lean-to, when I took out my blankets they promptly froze in the frigid winter air. I learned one thing then: when wet things are put in your pack, they'll be wet when you take them out! This did not dampen our hike. I had such fun. I said then, "If I ever get the chance, I'd like to hike the entire Appalachian Trail."

From 1945 until 1951, I always kept the thought of hiking the Appalachian Trail in the back of my mind. I knew I had to hold on to that dream until it was fulfilled as it was too exciting to let go. Meanwhile, life had to take another turn or two until 1951, the next time I would see the Appalachian Trail again.

In 1951, the Appalachian Trail was a continuous, marked wilderness footpath traversing mostly wilderness in fourteen states from Mt. Oglethorpe, Georgia to Mt. Katahdin, Maine. It extended more than 2,050 miles.

After I graduated from Georgia Tech, I took a sales job in training for a managerial position with a company. This job was not exactly what I wanted, maybe because I was restless for my biggest adventure to come. I continued to work there for several months while at the same time I quietly prepared for my Trail hike, knowing I had to quit my job to go on the hike. Since my future wife, Eugenia, was still in college, this seemed like the opportune time. I shared with her my secret plan to hike the entire Appalachian Trail. While she said she would miss me, Eugenia was excited for me and very encouraging.

I finally told my parents three days before I left that I was going hiking on the Trail, but I did not reveal that I planned to hike the entire Trail. I did not want my parents to worry. Only mildly surprised, they were very supportive and agreed to help me any way they could.

Some people hike the Trail because something bad happened to them such as a divorce or job loss, creating the desire for time away from civilization. Others hike to find solace after the death of a loved one. Today, many hike the Appalachian Trail for its unique socializing aspect, different from the 1950s when only fourteen thru-hikes were recorded.

The motivation for my thru-hike was purely to have a fun vacation and to be right in the middle of the natural beauty God created. With so many adventures already experienced, I felt prepared for this major undertaking and was not daunted by danger and the "what-ifs." I methodically planned every detail I could, but was ready to face whatever curve the Trail threw at me as part of the thrill.

Instead of a flashlight, I used this miner's carbide lamp that creates light by igniting the acetylene gas produced by combining calcium carbide and water within its chambers. The wide reflector helps to produce a bright, broad light. Photo by Gary W. Meek.

CHAPTER 11

Hiking Gear

During the winter preceding my Appalachian Trail hike I studied camping equipment catalogs. Walk-in outdoor equipment stores were not available like they are now. I ordered all my equipment by mail from various places. The L.L. Bean Company and World War II Army surplus stores supplied most of my hiking equipment.

I paid five dollars for a new WWII Army surplus steel frame ski trooper's rucksack to use as a backpack. I did not use the included white camouflage cover. I added soft wool sheepskin to the webbing shoulder pads and back band for comfort and protection. I had a lightweight down-filled Trapper Model sleeping bag from the Alaska Sleeping Bag Company, and my inflatable air pillow added great comfort.

I carried a quart canteen for water, a small Primus gasoline cook stove, matches and a canteen containing white gasoline for fuel. I also took a Boy Scout aluminum cook kit (minus the frying pan), Boy Scout pocket knife, fork, spoon, miner's carbide lamp, 35 mm Kodak camera, compass, toilet kit, Band-Aids, sewing kit, plastic poncho for rainwear and ground cloth, two T-shirts, small clothesline, Maine guide shoes from L.L. Bean Company, spare leather shoelaces, one-man canvas Boy Scout tent (no sewn-in floor or mosquito proofing), New Testament Bible, small L.L. Bean hatchet for cutting tent poles, and five yards of mosquito netting. I broke in the two pairs of shoes before starting my hike.

My backpack weighed about forty-five pounds when fully loaded. This is considered a heavy load for hikers today with the much lighter weight equipment readily available.

The gasoline powered Primus stove made in Sweden burns similar to a blowtorch. The gasoline is stored in a tank at the bottom of the stove. To fire the stove I opened the heat-regulating valve at the top of the tank then cupped my hands around the tank. The heat from my hands made the gas expand and flow into the burner above the tank. At this point, I lit a match and used it to ignite the burner.

The purchased stove came with a twelve-ounce metal container that supported the cooking pot just above the burner. I discarded this container. In its place I made and attached a lighter three-prong sturdy aluminum wire tripod to hold the cooking pot. The stove was supposed to burn white gasoline. The supply places I used along the Appalachian Trail did not sell it. I did not ask the storekeepers about needing white gas, thus avoiding the possible misconception that I was asking to buy the moonshine whiskey commonly called "White Lightning" frequently made at that time in the mountains. Instead I used regular gasoline, which worked satisfactorily.

Using the stove for all of my cooking, I never built a single campfire for any purpose. With the cook stove I could boil water in just five minutes, start to finish. This was certainly quicker than building a fire with wood, and I didn't have to search for dry wood every night.

On the Trail I cleaned my cooking pots and utensils after each use with S.O.S. steel wool soap pads. First I would immerse the equipment in the stream and swish them out with running stream water, or canteen water if necessary. With my fingers I scrubbed sand around inside the boiler and around the utensils to get rid of most of the food particles. Afterward I pinched off and used only a tiny piece of the S.O.S. pad each time for cleaning and discarded the used steel wool. By using this frugal method, only two S.O.S. pads were needed for the whole trip.

The miner's carbide light is a small lamp that miners formerly attached to their head gear. It utilizes calcium carbide in the bottom compartment and water in the top. The water is regulated to drip on the carbide, producing acetylene gas, which jets out in the center of a polished metal reflector. A built-in steel wheel when struck against the flint piece ignites the lamp. A match can be used as an alternate. When the acetylene is set afire, the reflected light illuminates an area large enough to set up camp. It provides a dull light, but enough to facilitate reading. The carbide came in granules that I kept in a rigid, waterproof, reusable container. A few granules would provide light for a couple of hours.

When inside shelters I sometimes used candles I found there, in addition to my carbide lamp. I never carried a flashlight because using the carbide lamp was considerably lighter, more efficient and required no batteries. I fell in love with using my lamp as a spelunker while in college.

My carbide lamp is currently displayed in the Visitors Center at Amicalola Falls State Park at the start of the Approach Trail to Springer Mountain. Now it is considered to be a "most unusual" item.

Under my Jones-type hat, I kept each day's guide material. I stored insect repellent, salt and matches in small screw-top metal 35 mm film containers. In my buttoned shirt pocket I carried an aluminum collapsible drinking cup and a Compak snakebite kit. Thankfully I never had to use the snakebite kit.

My hiking staff is a chinaberry stick I began carrying when I was twelve years old, so of course it had to make the long trip with me. It was a big help in climbing over steep slopes, pushing aside bushes, wading across streams and fighting off dogs.

I packed adhesive tape for first aid and poncho repair, wrapping the tape around one of my film containers to save the weight of the spool. Individual waterproof zippered or drawstring bags kept my food and the calcium carbide for my light. I would have loved to have had a plastic bag to protect my rolled-up sleeping bag but plastic bags were not yet in use. Freeze-dried foods, vibram shoe soles, cell phones and positioning devices came out later, too.

The type of food I carried depended on the distance between supply points. On short stretches I used some canned foods, but on long hauls I carried lightweight food such as dehydrated soup mixes, dehydrated potatoes, powdered milk, and hot chocolate mix. The potatoes were ordered from the L.L. Bean Company. I tried to eat three main meals a day out of the limited variety of foods.

One of my standbys was cornmeal cooked with water as a cereal and eaten with sugar, raisins and milk. My favorite breakfast included chocolate pudding. I would cook it after supper and let it cool during the night by putting the covered boiler in a spring. After animals tried to get to the pudding, I learned to keep it inside my tent overnight and it was fine in the morning.

I utilized no food or supply caches and did not arrange for anyone to meet me along the way. My parents mailed guidebooks and some of my supplies to me, but most of the time I bought supplies from stores near the Trail about once a week. After long stretches of basically eating just cornmeal when rations ran low, I would eat everything I could when I met up with civilization.

At stores I usually bought two loaves of bread and three jars of different kinds of preserves. I made these into preserve sandwiches, alternating the flavors as I carefully packed them back into the original bread wrappers. At meal time I usually consumed two or three sandwiches. Somehow these sandwiches always stayed fresh in the cool mountain air.

Between meals I would assign myself goals such as reaching a certain peak before eating a candy bar or package of salted nuts. My favorites were Babe Ruth and Hershey chocolate bars. Many spectacular views were enjoyed as I sat and munched a snack. Often I would find myself reading and rereading wrappers on the snacks. I guess I wanted to keep in touch with civilization.

I hiked with maps and guidebooks published by the Appalachian

Trail Conference. These enabled me to plan intelligently for each night's stopping place and for replenishing my food supply. Also I enjoyed hiking a section more when I knew something of its history and what to expect in the way of outstanding features. The guidebooks provided some of this valuable information.

Oil company automobile maps showed me where the Appalachian Trail crossed on highways. I would estimate in which direction would be the nearest walk to a store for food. Now listed in the Appalachian guidebook are the closest stores along the Appalachian Trail.

On my hike I wore Wigwam cushioned fiber 100 percent DuPont nylon socks made from crimpled nylon fiber, thousands of them twisted together to make the yarn. They were just as soft and easy on the feet as wool. My two pairs of these athletic socks made the 123-day trek without a single hole in either pair.

At the end of each day's hike I washed my feet and socks. The socks rarely dried during the night, so the next morning I would tie the damp socks to the outside of my pack to complete drying while I wore the other pair. With the exception of a small blister on the second day of my hike I had no trouble at all with my feet and used no foot powder or medication.

This experience I had with my Wigwam socks was mentioned in some of the articles published about my hike. After readers contacted me asking where socks like this were available, I did a little national advertising and sold more than 600 pairs at $1.19 each from mail orders.

I had three white duck cloth trousers from my WWII service in the U.S. Navy. I used one pair to sleep in and the other two pairs for hiking. Almost all of my equipment lasted the entire trail hike. I traveled as light as I could with the equipment available in those days and took good care of it.

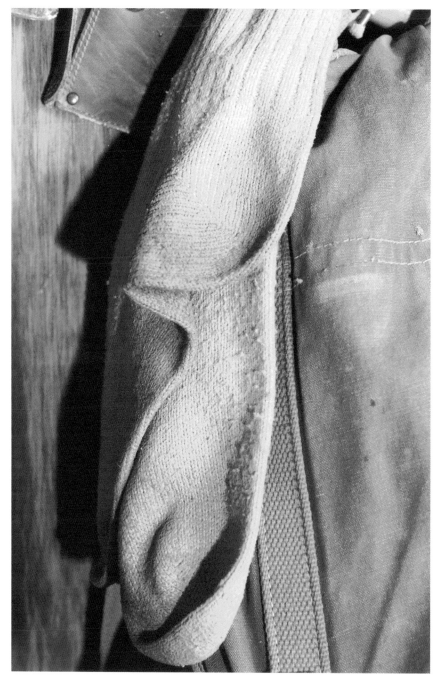

Two pairs of the Wigwam nylon athletic socks lasted the entire hike. Each day I wore one pair and washed the other pair which I tied to the outside of my backpack to dry as I hiked. Photo by Gary W. Meek.

CHAPTER 12
The Big Hike Begins

In May 1951, my hiking dream with all its preparation became a reality. At the age of twenty-four I started the "adventure of a lifetime" to Mount Katahdin along with a seventeen-year-old friend, a Life-ranked Boy Scout. Although we wanted to avoid the possibility of winter weather in Maine, we started a little later than the ideal time frame. To accommodate my friend's great desire to hike the Appalachian Trail, I waited until he graduated from high school.

We eagerly left Cordele dressed in our clean hiking clothes and carrying backpacks, and hitchhiked toward Tate, the nearest town to Mount Oglethorpe. The first night we only got to Canton outside Atlanta. There we pitched our tents in the front yard of a Georgia State Patrol post. No one said anything to us. The next morning we hitchhiked on into Tate, and from there we walked to Mount Oglethorpe.

In 1951, Mount Oglethorpe was in a remote, peaceful area. An unimproved road led to a weather-beaten, chipped marble statue of General James Oglethorpe, the founder of Georgia. The statue had been made by the Tate Marble Works.

A battered wooden sign got our attention as it read:

OGLETHORPE
SOUTHERN TERMINUS OF THE
APPALACHIAN TRAIL, A MOUNTAIN
FOOTPATH EXTENDING 2050 MILES
To MOUNT KATAHDIN IN MAINE

As we camped for the night near the top of Mount Oglethorpe, I was full of anticipation and happiness. I could hardly sleep for the hundred thoughts swirling in my head. Waking up on the beautiful sunny day of May 31, 1951, I was so excited to begin my glorious hike to Mount Katahdin. The next 123 days would turn out to be an even more incredible journey than I imagined that first day.

While breaking up our camp near the top of Mount Oglethorpe we met two Georgia Tech students as they started their hike. After breakfast we walked 3.5 miles on the Trail and found they had left us a surprise.

Even way back in my hiking days there was "trail magic" happening. "Trail magic" occurs when unexpected acts of hospitality are shown to Trail hikers. On this very first morning on the Appalachian Trail some "trail magic" appeared in the form of a surprise breakfast of fudge and cherry pie. What a great way to start the "big adventure!"

Despite such a good beginning, all the first day on the Trail my companion complained about his heavy backpack and the rough terrain. It was a struggle for both of us. For entertainment he repeatedly wanted to fire the 25-caliber pistol I carried in my holster.

He decided to just make it as far as Hot Springs, North Carolina. During the day his goal diminished to quitting at the North Carolina state line. Finally on the second day he had had enough and got off the Appalachian Trail at the next road he saw. He went back home and I continued alone, disappointed for him but understanding how hard the hike would have been for him. A few days after I returned home from my completed hike, my friend expressed to me his deep regret for ending his hike as he did.

On my second day I passed through Amicalola Falls State Park. There was nothing here but trees, rocks, water and a single-lane dirt road to the foot of the falls. I took a side trail to view the falls from the bottom. The constant whooshing sound of the rushing water lulled my mind as I stood mesmerized. It was a beautiful sight with the water sparkling in the sunshine as it cascaded down through the rocks and trees. It took effort to break away, but I knew there was much more to see on my journey.

Now the 1,020-acre park contains a 57-room lodge with restaurant and meeting facilities, rental cottages, picnic shelters, playgrounds, hiking trails, fishing pond, a visitors center building with outdoor exhibits, live reptiles, gift shop, and offices. Visitors can use steps and crosswalks to facilitate easy viewing of the beautiful 729-foot falls. In 2005 the Georgia Appalachian Trail Club and the Amicalola Falls State Park dedicated an Appalachian Trail exhibit in the visitor center. The exhibit includes information about maintaining and hiking the Appalachian Trail. My 1951 backpack and equipment I used are on display. A video continuously plays and shows a bit about my thru-hike as well as others talking about the Appalachian Trail.

At the end of the third day of my hike, I came to a fire tower on Hawk Mountain, Georgia. The tall wooden tower was made with four long logs as corner posts and an enclosed lookout cabin on top. Instead of steps, a metal vertical ladder rose up the center of the tower to a landing. Above the landing was a locked door into the cabin. The tower was torn down a few years later.

While still daylight I climbed up for a breathtaking 360-degree view of adjacent mountains. I enjoyed looking all around at God's beautiful handiwork in the inspiring scenery as the sun set.

I descended and found the nearby small locked ranger's cabin. I decided to sleep on the open four-foot-wide porch. Water was easily available at the spring down the mountain. I cooked some chocolate pudding from my mix and powdered milk and set it on the porch for the next day's breakfast. Before retiring I sat on the porch with my back to the wall with my light attached to an overhead nail and relaxed.

Feeling fortunate to have this great setup, I was writing in my diary when I heard bloodcurdling screams from nearby. I could not see anything out in the darkness. Apparently a pair of wildcats was attracted to the smell of my pudding. These wildcats were carrying on and carrying on. They were scratching and fighting and knocking down bushes at the edge of the clearing. Scared, I hastily put everything back in my pack and grabbed it along with the pudding, light, and hiking staff. I ran to the safety of the fire tower. Able somehow to hold on to everything while I made one trip up the ladder, I was fully determined not to make a second trip near the fray.

There were no sides to the approximately three-foot-wide landing. I spread out my sleeping bag and tied it to the platform with my shoelaces, belt and tent rope so I would not roll over and fall. I had a little trouble with the wind rocking the tower, but I didn't have any more trouble with the wildcats. I got into the sleeping bag, zipped up and had a good night's sleep – fifty feet up. And my chocolate pudding was as good as ever when I woke up.

From Hawk Mountain I descended gradually to Hightower Gap, the center of hunting and fishing activities in the Blue Ridge Wildlife Management Area in the Chattahoochee National Forest. I saw no one. The Appalachian Trail ascends following the ridgeline to the summit of Sassafras Mountain. I certainly observed some pretty views here, but saw no signs of U.S. Army Rangers training in this area as they frequently did in those years.

Late in the afternoon of June 3, I reached Woody Gap, named for the barefooted, legendary Arthur Woody. He started working as a forest ranger when the Chattahoochee National Forest was established. The beloved Ranger Woody did an outstanding job in fire prevention, timber management and game protection. Credited with creating the first wildlife management area in the South and reestablishing whitetail deer in the area, he passed away in 1946.

I cooked supper and enjoyed water flowing from a pipe. A car pulled up and several teenage girls got out. Their amused curiosity after catching me washing my feet in the water quickly turned to interest in my hike. They drove off and as a surprise, they later returned with some ice cream for me. I appreciated all the kind things people did for me all along my journey.

After sleeping on top of a picnic table, I hiked the next morning 1.6 miles into the little town of Suches, Georgia. I planned to visit the post office and a store.

There were a few things that I found I could do without so I wanted to mail them home to reduce my pack weight. Chief among these was my razor. I had not met any other hikers on the Trail. It was so unhandy shaving in the middle of the woods, I decided I could joyfully stop shaving. Beards were not popular at that time, and my having a beard probably did hurt me later in catching rides to stores. It was so worth it though! I mailed my items and replenished my supplies at a grocery store before catching a ride back to Woody Gap.

When I arrived at Blood Mountain I became interested in its history. Blood Mountain (4,461 feet) is the highest point on the Georgia section of the Trail. According to a Native American legend, a battle was fought on Blood Mountain between the Cherokees and Creeks that was so fierce the mountain ran red with blood. In the 1930s the Civilian Conservation Corps built a sturdy two-room stone hut on Blood Mountain. The nearest water is a third of a mile down the Trail.

Neel's Gap was interesting as it featured the now-defunct Walasi-Yi Inn, a hotel for tourists. At the time I passed through, state prisoners were busy getting the inn ready for the summer season. Today the area buzzes with activity related to the Mountain Crossings store at Walasi-Yi. The English translation of the Cherokee name, Walasi-Yi, means "Place of the Frogs." It is the only place on the Trail route that the Appalachian Trail actually passes through part of a building.

I started out wearing a U.S. Navy fatigue shirt of chambray material, but along the trail before Unicoi Gap the thorny vines ripped the sleeves to shreds during the first week.

I went off the trail to Helen, Georgia, to replace my tattered shirt and to repair a rip in the lining of my sleeping bag. Some idea of my determination to hike the entire Trail may be gained from an article that appeared in the *Tri-County Advertiser*, Clarkesville, Georgia:

"According to Robert Taylor of Helen, Georgia, Eugene M. Espy is not only an excellent hiker, but he doesn't forget promises made along the way. Mr. Espy is the young man from Cordele, Georgia, who is hiking the Appalachian Trail, every natural-born step of it. When Mr. Espy reached Unicoi Gap he made a detour to Helen.

"The young man asked Mr. Taylor for directions to a seamstress who could mend his sleeping bag. Mr. Taylor says, 'I told him, and then I gave him some free advice. First, I told him he'd best go home to his mother. And when I saw he was of no mind to take that advice, I told him how he could short-cut up here to Tray Mountain and avoid going back to Unicoi. I saw he was of no mind to take this advice either, so I told him if he ever really made it to Katahdin to please let me know. Well, sir, I got a postcard from Millinocket, Maine, dated October 1, saying he had completed his hike the day before.' "

The Army twill shirt I bought in Helen lasted the rest of my hike. The sleeves did hold up, but the back became worn clean through in places from the frame and straps of my pack. My Navy-issued white trousers were ideal for the journey. The trousers now are a gray, dingy color, yet are perfectly preserved. Although the pant legs are tattered at the bottom, there are no holes. I knew the duck material wouldn't get snagged from thorny vines, trees, or rocks.

Throughout Georgia I encountered a lot of rain. My poncho kept my body reasonably dry, but my feet and legs became soaked and cold. One day as I continued on, I became so cold and wet from the wind and rain that the muscles of my right knee stiffened. Walking became increasingly difficult and agonizing. When I reached Plum Orchard Gap in the late afternoon of June 7, I'd had about all I could take.

I knew I couldn't go on without a break. My tent had been mailed to Damascus, Virginia, and I didn't feel up to sitting through a long night crouched under my poncho.

My perseverance cranking up to a crescendo, I hiked down the mountain on a side trail for a mile and a half until I came to the isolated home of Hoke Eller and his family. They mostly raised chickens on their simple mountainside farm. I asked if I could please sleep in a barn or any place to get out of the rain. After the farmer found out I wasn't a hobo, he opened up his home to my weary body.

The Eller family was exceptionally kind to me. They took me in, fed me supper, and built a fire in the open fireplace so I could dry my clothes. When bedtime came, they let me sleep on a cot in the attic. I was awakened during the night by the loud rat-a-tat sound of hail pounding the tin roof a few inches above my head. This home had electricity, and their water was piped into the house from a spring high up in the mountains. The sink faucet was always left running. After a good breakfast with these fine people I returned to the trail. Thankfully, the weather was clear for a while that day.

By the time I reached Deep Gap a cold rain was coming down in such torrents that it obscured the Trail and its markings. Big muddy puddles greeted almost every step, inviting me to slide into them. I decided to lay over a day during these heavy rains and take a rest like the forest animals. It would be one of only six days off for me on the entire hike of 123 days. I enjoyed reading my Bible and lounging in the cozy lean-to there. The meditation in the quiet place relaxed my mind and my body and provided respite from the constant "trudging on."

I was surprised when a Nantahala National Forest ranger drove up in a jeep. He got out and politely asked why I was in the shelter. I could tell that he was not accustomed to seeing hikers. He was very interested in my hike and well-being.

Then the ranger raised an eyebrow and asked, "You are not carrying any kind of firearm, are you?" I told him about the pistol I had in the bottom of my pack and showed him my Georgia pistol toter's license to carry it. I had needlessly brought it along for possible protection against wildlife. The pistol had been getting rained on in the holster on my belt, so I had stored it inside my pack. Since firearms could not be mailed, I planned to send it home by express when I reached Hot Springs, North Carolina.

He got a bit upset that there was a prohibited firearm in his National Forest, but he understood my situation. He applied a seal to the pistol and said, "Maybe that will keep you out of trouble when you hike through to the Smoky Mountains. Say, why don't you leave your pack at the Deep Gap shelter so I can move it to the next lean-to for you?" I eagerly accepted his offer so I could hike the 21-mile Albert Mountain trail section without carrying my pack.

After spending the night at Deep Gap, I joyfully left my pack for the ranger. That morning I had beautiful weather as I hiked in the Nantahala Mountains, one of the most magnificent portions of the Appalachian Trail. From the fire tower on Standing Indian Mountain, the views in all directions were extraordinary. About twelve miles farther along the Trail I saw more grand views from Albert Mountain. I ended this glorious day at Wallace Gap, where I left the Trail and hiked to the White Oak Bottoms lean-to.

There I found my pack with an attached note from the ranger. The ranger's house was nearby, and he invited me to be his guest for a dinner of delicious mountain trout. I slept well with my full stomach that night of June 10.

The lean-tos, or trail shelters, in 1951, were constructed with three sides and a roof. One side was open and unprotected. All had dirt floors, but none had outhouses or privies. The Civilian Conservation Corps made shelters in the Smoky Mountains that had continuous side-by-side bunks made of wire netting. The shelters offered no protection from animals such as bears, which were prevalent in the Smokies.

Sometime before my thru-hike, my brother, John Lee, and a buddy were sitting with their packs in a Smoky Mountain trail shelter. A bear ran them off and raided their packs of all the food. All other items remained except for their flashlight. John Lee suggested that on my trek through the Smokies I should be on the lookout for a bear running around with his flashlight.

Years after my thru-hike, protective bear fences were installed on the shelters. Some years later these were removed due to concerns for hikers' safety. Hikers inside the shelters had fed bears through the fencing, thus creating a dangerous situation as often bears would visit expecting handouts of food.

Now, some trail shelters have plank tables and a sleeping frame of wire netting. Cast iron stoves are found in some of the shelters in New England. Metal bear poles with cross-arms to suspend packs beyond reach of bears have been installed at some overnight sites.

As I camped out all along the Trail before retiring for the night I stacked firewood or stones near where I slept. If anything scared me I would throw the stones or firewood in that direction. After extinguishing my light I would sit up, tense as I watched and listened as the nearby wildlife settled for the night. The woods became quiet, and then I heard the crickets, owls, and various other animals amid the rustling of the wind in the trees. I enjoyed the peace, but I stayed ready for any action.

Hiking in Wesser Canyon, I passed a broken overshot water wheel, the only remains of an old mill. The highway I crossed at Wesser, North Carolina, was wilderness. A steel bridge spanned the Nantahala River with the dirt road turning east at an ancient but still operating country store. The Wesser Post Office occupied one corner. Several years later the store closed.

Nowadays Wesser is a beehive of activity with stores, restaurants, and outdoor centers. The Nantahala is filled with rented boats and paraphernalia floating down the river.

On June 16, I reached the Silers Bald Trail Shelter in the Great Smoky Mountains. While preparing to spend the night, I found a note signed by the assistant scoutmaster of a troop that spent the previous night in the shelter. The note read: "To the next occupant: When the sun goes behind the hills and darkness descends upon this lean-to, beware of Lardbutt, the Silers Bald bear."

The note went on to describe the Scouts' experience. Despite their efforts to scare the bear off by shooting firecrackers and banging tin plates, the bear harassed them all night long. It stole and ate four pounds of their lard (rendered hog fat), two pounds of margarine, and several loaves of bread. The lean-to was built close to the steep mountainside, and the bear climbed up the mountain onto the weak roof. The Scouts expected the bear to come crashing through the roof onto them at any minute, so they spent a sleepless night.

I had heard many stories about bears in the Smokies, and this note shook me up a bit as I had read what Lardbutt had done to the Scouts and their possessions. I anticipated a long night of tangling with Ol' Lardbutt, but as it turned out I enjoyed a quiet night without seeing him.

Two days later I arrived at the Hughes Ridge shelter for the night. After I got through cooking supper I went way down some distance to a spring and washed my pots and pans. All of a sudden I heard something rumbling around up at the lean-to. I just knew a bear had gotten into my pack. I beat my pots and pans and hollered all the way back as I was running to the lean-to. I got up there and realized with a sigh of relief it was all peace and quiet at the lean-to.

The next morning, however, I was inside the shelter getting ready to leave when a black bear came lumbering slowly along from left to right about six feet from me. What an interesting sight, I thought, as I slowly caught my breath. I was relieved that this bear along with three others I saw in the Smokies never gave me any trouble.

Several years later a hiker from Knoxville, Tennessee, planned to spend the night at the Hughes Ridge shelter he had used on a previous hike. It was a week after a bad snowstorm, and he was having difficulty finding the shelter. Finally, the hiker discovered the charred remains of the shelter and the body of a man in the snow.

The hiker contacted the Great Smoky Mountains National Park, prompting two rangers to come in a jeep to the site. One of the rangers turned the body over and quickly recognized it. He said, "Why, that's Ol' Joe!" He was an elderly Cherokee Indian well-known for carrying moonshine whiskey from Tennessee across the Smokies into the Native American reservation of Cherokee, North Carolina. Cherokee was legally dry, which meant no alcohol could be sold or consumed.

The rangers could tell that some of the moonshine that he was carrying had been consumed. The old Cherokee in his drunken condition must have set fire to the shelter to keep warm. The shelter has never been rebuilt.

About a week later in Tennessee, I met a man carrying a load of moonshine whiskey. His moonshine containers had been rolled up in a piece of canvas and the ends then tied together to make a horse collar pack. I was frightened he would think I was a revenue officer, or that I might report him to the authorities. I told him I was not from around that part of the country. I emphasized I was just walking through on the "government trail." The moonshiner put his pack down and said, "Well, partner. Let's have a drink!" I didn't want to drink any moonshine. Not wanting to hurt his feelings, I told him, "You go ahead. I've got a long way to go, you know. You go ahead, though." He seemed satisfied with my explanation and said he would have a drink anyway. I left him there drinking.

I later noticed several places in that area laced with lots of little streams that would be a good place to have a still to make moonshine, if one were so inclined. In my mind, I could picture a still and a moonshiner's rifle pointed at me following my every step. Thus motivated, I did not look to the right or to the left. "Hear no evil. See no evil." For several miles I kept my head looking straight forward as I hiked, seeing only nature at its best. At the time I hiked the Appalachian Trail, it was so remote, especially in Tennessee, that moonshiners felt comfortable in making and moving their highly illegal, but profitable, "home-grown" whiskey. Due to their scarcity, hikers were automatically scrutinized with a wary eye by locals as possibly being outsiders "up to something."

Several times I would hike for a hundred yards or so along a stream with thick rhododendron blooms on either side of me. In the South the rhododendrons and flame azaleas were some of the most beautiful and prominent plants I saw. The explosion of bright colors in contrast to the various shades of green in the woods was a stunning sight. This bit of cheer was always welcome. I learned that when plants bloomed in the valley it would be about six weeks before the same plants bloomed at the top of the mountains.

The Appalachian Trail is officially marked with two-inch-by-six-inch white blazes painted on tree trunks, boulders, wooden stakes, fences, and telephone poles. A few small diamond-shaped ATC metal markers are used. The goal when hiking the Appalachian Trail is to have a marking always within sight.

I encountered deplorable conditions in many places along the Trail in 1951. The blazes had deteriorated or been obscured. The poor Trail conditions had been intensified by severe hurricanes and ice storms, natural summer growth, and blowdowns. Logging had severely damaged some of the trailway. Trail markers were often missing, deteriorated, or grown over. Some spots I encountered were so rugged that they had to be climbed on my hands and knees.

In the South, the natural growth of bushes, limbs and thorny vines had taken over the Trail in some places, making the path difficult to follow. I had to bushwhack to get through.

Beautiful rhododendrons often line the Appalachian Trail in North Carolina. The center of this 1951 photo shows the Trail was overgrown and difficult to follow sometimes.

The rough Trail situation was also partly due to the fact that during World War II, Appalachian Trail activities in the South practically ceased. Privately owned Trail lands in the southern Appalachians were beyond the resources of trail workers. After World War II, limited maintenance resumed in certain sections. Today, with many more volunteers, a much bigger effort is made to maintain the Trail.

There were no trees growing on Big Bald Mountain in North Carolina, just wild grass nearly waist high, hence, the name. There was no path or sign of the Trail. As I hiked along I kept looking in the distance for a possible trail route through an opening where trees picked up. As I walked I used my hiking staff to partially open up a hole in the high grass.

I nearly stepped right on a four-foot-long timber rattlesnake. A surge of raw fear shot through my body. It's okay, I told myself as I tried to remain focused.

As the snake coiled up to strike, I stepped back, making sure I did not step on his brother. With my staff I separated the grass to get a good opening to kill it with my staff. I drew back my staff above my head and took a deep breath. WHA-A-AP! I hit the snake with such force my staff broke! The rattler disappeared into the weeds, but I went after it and finished it off with the larger part of my broken staff.

My precious hiking stick had now shrunk from four and a half feet to three and a half feet in length. I rounded the broken end of my wooden staff and it went on to Mount Katahdin with me.

A few times as I was walking in short grass I would see the body of a snake that I had just stepped over. I didn't know where its head or tail was, so I just kept walking to avoid a confrontation.

I observed more snakes than many hikers in recent years have reported. I only killed the poisonous ones in my way. I learned to identify snakes when I was a Boy Scout. After careful observation, I killed about fifteen rattlesnakes, the largest of which was the four-foot timber rattler. The last rattlesnake I killed was on Jug End Mountain in Massachusetts. Whenever I came to a blown-down log, I made sure I stepped on the log before taking a long step beyond the log in case there was a snake stretched out next to it on the other side.

In Pennsylvania I used my trusty staff to kill five copperheads, the only poisonous snakes I saw in that state. In fact, Pennsylvania was the one place on the Appalachian Trail where I saw copperheads.

In addition to killing snakes, my staff helped keep me balanced when I was hiking or jumping from rock to rock when crossing streams. A couple of times I used it to fight off attacks from dogs. Now my staff is prominently displayed on the wall of our den.

One time my hiking stick let me down, though. The north side of Three Ridges in Virginia was grown up in waist-high ferns. I was coming down a steady descent at a good pace, making a half-hearted attempt to spread the ferns aside with my stick. I didn't see the trunk of a fallen tree laying across the trail. My feet hit the tree and I fell forward as if I had been tackled. The bottom end of my stick jammed into the ground and the top end caught me in the stomach, catapulting me up and over. I came down on my head. Fortunately, I kept each day's guidebook data under my hat. That habit saved my skull. The first thing I did as I stood upright was hold my watch to my ear to see if it was still ticking. It was!

Having a working watch was most important. Knowing how many hours of daylight remained enabled me to effectively plan rest stops, lunch breaks, and stopping places for the night. Without having a watch, the clouds, rain, and fog would have made it difficult to determine the time of day.

I had a few falls on my hike, but none serious. Whenever I stepped onto wet leaves on a flat rock, I was particularly careful.

I met very few people on the Appalachian Trail, several times going a week without seeing anyone. People just were not hiking. I could have been seriously injured any number of ways, and weeks maybe months might pass before any help would have come along. This is certainly different from today's sometimes "crowded" Trail.

I had difficulty following the Trail between Devil's Fork Gap and Spivey's Gap. The area was dense and overgrown with brush. I encountered frequent blowdowns and few visible markings which necessitated me bushwhacking most of this section.

On June 24, I spent the night in a farmer's hayloft. This was one of the few times I did not get invited to sleep in the family's home. I was grateful, anyway, for the shelter.

The aluminum pan and cup were used for eating and drinking on the Trail. Photo by Gary W. Meek.

CHAPTER 13

Damascus Hospitality

The Appalachian Trail led right through the small town of Damascus in southwestern Virginia. When I hiked into Damascus on June 28, I entered Corney's Place, the only eating establishment I saw in this town of about 1,200 people. Feeling hungry for a good lunch, I walked past several tables in the restaurant/store and sat on one of the round stools at the bar. I put my pack on the floor at my feet. I ordered an astounding ten slices of toast with syrup and a chocolate milkshake.

As I was enjoying this feast, a man wearing dark trousers and a white shirt sat down on the stool beside me. He asked me, "What are you doing in Damascus?" I told him I had started in Georgia and was hiking the Appalachian Trail all the way to Maine. We talked a minute or two and then he left me.

A few minutes later he came back and said he had called the editor of the *Washington County News* in Abingdon, Virginia. The newspaper editor wanted to talk to me if I didn't mind. I said sure, that I would be happy to talk to her. He directed me to the wall telephone with the receiver hanging down and left the restaurant. I told the editor about my hike and gave her my Georgia address. She published her article and mailed that edition of the newspaper to Cordele for me to read upon my return.

Having not yet been given a bill, I asked my waitress how much I owed. The waitress/cashier cheerfully said with a big smile, "Not a thing! The chief said you were okay!" She explained that the man with whom I had been talking was Chief "Corney" McNish, the

Appalachian Trail Hiker Stops Off In Damascus

Damascus is one of the few towns that the historic Appalachian Trail goes through in its two-thousand mile journey, and that is why Eugene Espy stopped to talk to Damascus people Thursday.

Espy, a 24 year-old graduate of Georgia Tech, started out May 31 to hike the trail from Georgia to Maine, and he figured he had covered about 400 miles when he hit Damascus. A friend started with him, but gave up after lugging the 45 pound pack up hill about 4 miles.

Espy carries tent, sleeping bag, small stove and plenty of dehydrated food in his pack, he said. He studies guide books and markers to follow the trail, which was for the most part a wilderness footpath, he said. He thought the trail would follow mountain ranges for the greatest part of the distance to Maine.

Espy said he was not particularly tired and that he expected to reach the end of the trail some time in September. He said it had been a "pretty rough trip." There were lots of snakes in the Smokies and he had seen six bears. "The bears won't hurt you, he said, "but they will steal your food if they get a chance."

Espy's home is in Cordele, Georgia, and it was at Mt. Oglethorpe, Georgia, that he set out on the trail.

Chief "Corney" McNish posed with me as he proudly showed me around his town of Damascus, Virginia, on June 28, 1951. The *Washington County News* article resulted from a telephone interview with me as I ate in Chief McNish's restaurant, Corney's Place.

Damascus police chief. Pointing out his wife, Gladys, working in the restaurant, she informed me that the police chief and his wife owned the restaurant.

Chief McNish returned to the store in time for me to thank him. I then accepted his invitation to ride in the police car to see the sights around town. He seemed so proud to show me around. He took a camera and film out of the store stock and shot lots of pictures of us. Damascus was a nice little town.

Earlier I had told Chief McNish that Damascus was a mail stop for me. I planned to pick up a package and send out some picture postcards. When we returned to the store, he plucked a handful of postcards from his sales rack. He kindly told me to address them to my friends, then give the cards back to him for stamping and mailing. He said, "You have a long way to go and need to save your money."

I sat at one of his tables and pulled out my short, stubby pencil. Chief McNish took two new pencils out of his sales stock, sharpened them, and gave them to me. He suggested I leave my backpack at the table and make myself at home, saying, "Make the store your headquarters for anything you need." I spent the rest of the day eating his treats and writing cards.

Afterward, I walked down the street to the post office and picked up my tent, dehydrated cubed potatoes, and new guidebook material. I removed some of the potatoes and mailed the rest to another post office about 400 miles up the Appalachian Trail.

By this time, it was getting late in the afternoon, and I prepared to leave Damascus. The sky was looking like rain. A storm was brewing. The chief approached on the sidewalk, asking me where I was going to sleep that night. I told him I would hike a few more miles and pitch my tent. He said, "Come on and sleep down at headquarters and get an early start in the morning."

Well, "headquarters" turned out to be the new town jail, the only public accommodation in Damascus. I had never seen a jail before, but it looked just like in the movies. The steel boiler plate bunk was attached to the wall with chains supporting both ends. There was a special prison-issue toilet without a lid. The chief told the jailer to bring something soft to cover the hard bunk. I put my sleeping bag on top of the blankets he supplied.

Chief McNish handed me a note that read, "Give this man what he wants for breakfast. He is OK." My stomach did a few happy leaps. I did look forward to a big free breakfast! It sure beat my usual corn meal mush.

I washed my clothes in the sink in the cell and hung them to dry on my clothesline strung between the bars of my unlocked cell. I slept just fine; no one else was there. I had never been in jail, but being an invited guest was pretty good.

The next morning I just handed my note to the waitress at Corney's Place as I plopped on the stool and started ordering. I eagerly ate one order of grits, toast, ham, two eggs, and milk. The waitress leaned in and asked, "How was it?" I replied, "Real good." With a wide smile brimming with hospitality, she offered, "Want more?" My face lit up as I nodded, and she brought me more. After the second round, she asked again. I agreed to more, finally putting away a total of three orders of each. I think that was the biggest meal I have ever eaten then — or since.

Oh, the joys of trail life. With renewed energy, I started off again on the Appalachian Trail, knowing that the people of Damascus, Virginia, had won a special place in my heart.

In 1954 I married and drove on our honeymoon through Damascus, where I introduced my bride to Chief McNish. He gave me a photograph that he had taken of Dr. George F. Miller, the 72-year-old, umbrella-toting, retired professor who was a thru-hiker of the Appalachian Trail in 1952.

On a subsequent visit, I learned that Orville "Corney" McNish became a deputy sheriff and was tragically killed in the line of duty.

In 1960, a man shot his estranged wife and two relatives. With his young children as hostages in his home, he held off a large group of state troopers and deputies. Deputy McNish was said to have been talking to the man in an effort to get him to surrender. McNish was fatally shot by the man, who then committed suicide.

I'm with Damascus Town Councilman Charles Trivett (right) and Alice Trivett (on porch).

In 1975, the Damascus United Methodist Church purchased a house directly behind the sanctuary. The church intended to level the building, vacant for 20 years, for a parking lot.

Then Postmaster Pascal Grindstaff stepped in as the hero with foresight. He saw the increasing number of hikers and bicyclists in Damascus. "No Appalachian town should be complete without a hostel," he said. He persuaded the parishioners that a hostel for Trail hikers and Virginia Creeper bicyclists would be more appropriate.

With the help of Town Councilman Charles Trivett and Alice Trivett, the old house was renovated. Separate bath facilities for males and females were installed. New kitchen appliances were purchased.

"The Place," as it is called, opened its doors in 1975. Hundreds and hundreds of hikers and bicyclists have enjoyed using it.

In 1979, John Harmon, a journalist by profession, hiked from Springer Mountain to Shenandoah National Park, then hitchhiked to Mount Katahdin and hiked back South to Shenandoah. I did not know of him until I heard him speak to the Georgia Wilderness Society about his hike of the Trail. After this meeting, I introduced myself. He had me repeat my name.

Harmon then pulled out a *Florida Times Union/Jacksonville Journal* newspaper and pointed out a paragraph he had written about me. The newspaper had sponsored Harmon in order for him to send back articles about the Trail. He stayed at "The Place" hostel while in Damascus. Gladys McNish, Chief McNish's widow, lived next door. When they met and she found out he was from Georgia, she had him read my story, included in the two-volume set of Rodale Press books, *Hiking the Appalachian Trail.* I had sent these to her earlier.

Newspaper Article Written by John Harmon:

A plump white-haired woman sways in a rocker on a century old porch. The sun shines darts of light through the tree-lined street.

She turns her head, eyes greeting a hiker as he and backpack come methodically up the sidewalk.

"How far have you come?" she asks with a shout.

"I started at Springer Mountain, Georgia," the 20ish man replies. "That's over 430 miles through some of the roughest mountains between here and there."

"Well, son, I'd say you deserve a rest. Let me be the first to welcome you to Damascus – the friendliest town on the Appalachian Trail."

With the white blaze markers of the Appalachian Trail running straight out of the mountains and down Main Street, hikers are no rare sight to the folks of Damascus. Extending a friendly hand to weary backpackers is a tradition that this small town, a mile from the Tennessee line, is proud of. It's a tradition that grows with each seasonal wave of long distance hikers.

I (left) stand with my backpack and staff in front of "The Place" hostel in Damascus, Virginia, during the First Trail Days in 1987.

Eugenia and I visited Gladys McNish once while she lived next door to "The Place." Each Christmas we mailed her a card with an enclosed twenty dollar bill, a token of my eternal gratitude for a warm welcome.

In 1987, the fiftieth anniversary celebration of completion of the Appalachian Trail program was held in the front yard of "The Place" in conjunction with the "First Annual Appalachian Trail Days Celebration," an event that continues in a big way today. Dan "Wingfoot" Bruce, a seven-time thru-hiker of the entire Trail, and I were included as speakers. I marched in the parade and displayed my backpack and hiking equipment on a picnic table in front of "The Place." That night a film and lecture on the Appalachian Trail was given by Warren Doyle, a thru-hiker of the Trail many times.

At the end of the parade a National Geographic Society photographer asked to take my picture for use in a book about the Trail. I told him the book, The Appalachian Trail, which the society published back in the early 1970s, had many pages of places that had nothing to do with the Appalachian Trail. I said I hoped the forthcoming book would stick more to the Trail itself. He pointed out a man in the distance as being editor of both the one I was referring to and the new book. I mentioned to this editor how I felt.

In 1988, the National Geographic Society did indeed adhere to the Trail in its new book, Mountain Adventure. This edition had a picture of me standing in front of "The Place."

During the 1987 Trail Days, I gave a two-volume set of the Rodale Press books about the Appalachian Trail to the Damascus Public Library in memory of "Corney" McNish. Also I presented two framed exhibits of the experiences of some of the early hikers passing through Damascus. These frames are mounted on the wall of the entrance to the Town Hall.

In 2008, I spoke at the Twenty-Second Appalachian Trail Days Festival. Since the first Trail Days Festival in 1987, the number of visitors has grown from a few hundred to more than 25,000. People come from all over to Damascus, "The Friendliest Town on the Trail." Damascus now has several outdoor outfitters and businesses related to hiking, bicycling, and fishing. The once-serious Trail Days parade is now enlivened by people shooting water out of squirt guns at each other and throwing balloons filled with water.

I sometimes think about how times have changed in Damascus. In 1951, hikers were scarce. When the police chief saw me with my backpack, he had to ask me why I was in town. For years now, everyone there has recognized hikers passing through Damascus. Having a police chief like Chief "Corney" McNish and a postmaster like Pascal Grindstaff was the town's first step in being known as friendly.

I (left) walk with my hiking staff in the First Annual Appalachian Trail Days celebration parade in Damascus, Virginia, in 1987.

I carried this Compak snakebite kit in my shirt pocket at all times while on the Trail. Thankfully I never had to use it. Photo by Gary W. Meek.

CHAPTER 14

Good People and Good Food

In the southern part of Virginia, there were 250 miles of Appalachian Trail with no lean-tos or shelters of any kind for hikers. I camped out in my tent many of the nights there. In 1951, there were no hiker hostels anywhere on the Trail.

All along the way people were good to me. On several occasions in sections where the country was largely agricultural, I asked farmers if I could sleep in their haylofts or outbuildings.

The farm families would not only allow me to stay in an outbuilding, they would invite me to join them for supper and breakfast. Because my arrival was unexpected, I shared the meals they had planned for themselves. Breakfast in these homes featured home-sliced bacon (streak of lean and streak of fat) and biscuits with the thickest white gravy I had ever seen.

At mealtimes there would be interesting conversations. One question that was always asked was, "Why are you hiking the Trail?" In turn I asked questions or made comments about farming. When it came time to retire, I usually ended up in a bed in the home not an outbuilding.

I sensed that most of these people in southern Virginia were good, hardworking people – poor but certainly generous. Some homes had no electricity, no window screens, and no indoor plumbing. No one would accept remuneration. Sometimes I would slip a couple of dollar bills under my breakfast plate and silently hope they would apply the money toward the installation of screens to fight the myriads of flies.

I carried a large cloth sign that I had made before I left home. It read, "Appalachian Trail Club Hikers." I used this to assist in catching rides from the Trail highway crossing to a store down the road. I quit displaying this after finding out most drivers did not know about the Appalachian Trail. A few thought of it as the "Government Trail."

This homemade cloth hiker sign that I carried to help me catch rides to and from stores was useless as no motorists seemed to know what the Appalachian Trail was in 1951. I eventually sent it home.

Sometimes non-hikers that I met would ask, "How much are they paying you to hike that government trail?" I asked them, "Who do you think would be paying me?" They'd say, "The government or somebody. Surely you must be receiving money from somewhere." Then I'd tell them, "No one is paying me. This is my vacation." Some would remark, "Go-o-lle-e!" Others would say, "They couldn't pay me enough to do that!"

The first day after leaving Damascus I encountered a bad thunderstorm. I stopped at a farmhouse and asked permission to stay overnight in an outbuilding. The owner refused. I felt somewhat rejected, but I could understand why they refused me. My appearance probably made them uncomfortable. By this time I had a beard, which was uncommon in 1951, and my clothes were tattered. This was the only time I was refused permission to stay at a farm outbuilding.

I continued on in the rain. I was glad I had picked up my tent in Damascus as I really needed it now. On June 29, I reached Sculls Gap, Virginia, where I pitched my tent and prepared my food in the pouring rain.

The Appalachian Trail went east from Damascus and followed along the New River. As per the guide instructions, a local farmer paddled me across the river in his small boat for free. He had seen very, very few hikers and was curious about my hike. The Trail looped down into North Carolina for a few miles then back up to Farmers Mountain, overlooking Byllesby Dam on the New River.

In Virginia it passed through Galax and Fancy Gap and continued eastward into the Dan River Canyon and over the Pinnacles of Dan. It dropped so steeply that I actually slid and rolled part of the way. The slickness of the Trail, caused by recent rains, made it extremely difficult to descend safely from the Pinnacles, wade across the river, and then climb back out of the steep-sided canyon.

The Pinnacles of Dan are sheer rock cones rising almost a thousand feet from the floor of the Dan River Gorge. These scenic formations presented the Appalachian Trail's most difficult traverse. Since I made my hike, the Trail has been rerouted around this area. That is good because the Appalachian Trail is supposed to be a hiking trail not a rock-climbing adventure.

Earl Shaffer once told me about how the Trail got routed over the Pinnacles of Dan. Years ago, Myron Avery led his small group on a scouting trip to route the Trail in this area. As a practical joke, some of the hikers ahead of Avery routed the Trail over the Pinnacles. Instead of rejecting this most difficult route, Avery approved it and said, "Let's mark it!" Many are glad the Trail has been relocated far away from these conical mountains.

I spent the night of July 4 at the home of John Barnard, keeper of the Appalachian Trail through the rugged Pinnacles of Dan section. Nothing was mentioned about it being the national holiday. The elderly Barnard and his wife were small dairy farmers. He showed me around his well-kept farm, which was run without modern conveniences. After each milking he put the milk cans in a spring house as he did not have electricity. Every morning he placed the full cans for pickup at a nearby road. The dairy distributor picked up the milk and dropped off clean, empty cans for reuse.

Barnard showed me some newspaper articles about Appalachian Trail hikers. It was here that I first read about the thru-hiker Earl Shaffer and his conquest of the Trail in 1948. I was surprised to learn that up to that time Shaffer was the only person who had hiked the Appalachian Trail in one continuous effort. Hearing about his hike being the first thru-hike made no difference to me. I was hiking purely for my personal satisfaction and entertainment and not trying to set any record. I had my own goal to hike every mile of the Appalachian Trail from Mount Oglethorpe to Mount Katahdin, enjoying it and exploring all interesting side trails.

I continued hiking on in Virginia. On one occasion after spending the night in an outbuilding, a mountain family filled my canteen with milk before I left. After a couple of hours of hiking I stopped to enjoy this much anticipated refreshment. When I turned up the canteen I felt soft lumps fill my mouth. I thought I had swallowed a cockroach! After recovering from my panic, I discovered that the milk had churned into butter as I walked along. Disappointed, I poured it out. It never occurred to me that one could churn milk to butter by hiking.

Along the Trail in Virginia, I stopped at one point to enjoy some beautiful mountain scenery. As I looked below, there were two women in long skirts washing clothes or perhaps making soap. A fire was under two big, black iron wash pots in which the contents were being stirred.

Mountain people were most interesting. Their lifestyle was quite different and sometimes I felt like I was witnessing life decades earlier. I quickly developed a healthy respect for the grit and determination these people possessed to meet their daily needs in the often harsh conditions.

Late one afternoon on July 11, near Parkers Gap Road, I met a truck carrying three men and a load of logs they had cut. They offered me a ride to a country store. I climbed on the back of the truck and secured my pack to one of the stanchions holding the logs. It was a breathtaking ride down that unimproved mountain road. I don't think the truck had any brakes. I was too busy holding on and dodging overhanging tree limbs to see much of the landscape. Finally the truck stopped at a store near Natural Bridge Station, Virginia.

At the store I bought some chocolate pudding mix and milk. Nearby, I cooked the pudding on my Primus stove and drank a couple of Coca-Colas. While the pudding was cooling, I returned to the store for a couple of bananas and a pint of vanilla ice cream. I added these to the pudding and indulged myself. I enjoyed the feast, but later I was very sick, probably from the rich food. After that I was more careful of what I ate, and that was the only time I was sick on my hike.

After a while I was able to walk down the country road to find a suitable place to pitch my tent nearby. I set up camp on the edge of a field near the road. After I had bedded down for the night, a drunk drove his car up close to my tent. He and I didn't hit it off too well. He insisted I was a draft-dodging Communist and felt duty bound to harass me. He threatened, "If I come back here and you're still here, I'll run over you!"

I stayed quiet to avoid further agitation from him and struggled to somehow suppress a desire to hit him over the head with my hiking stick. When he finally left, I found another camping location quickly and did not have any more trouble. Shortly after daybreak the next morning, I caught a ride back to the Appalachian Trail with the woodcutters. I knew after that encounter that I would need to be more careful not to pitch my tent near a public road.

After crossing the James River, the Trail ascended Bluff Mountain. While resting on a rock, I heard a rustling in the leaves behind me. I slipped out of my pack and silently moved toward the sound. As I looked through the undergrowth, I saw two small bears playing in a little sun-dappled clearing. When they saw me, they raced to a tree. One cub climbed to the fork of the first limb. The other climbed up on the trunk until it was about five feet from the ground, then stopped and stared at me. I was ten yards away and for a few seconds none of us moved. Then, as I took a step closer, the bear on the trunk climbed a bit higher. I stopped advancing, and he stopped climbing. This occurred repeatedly several times. It was a humorous situation, especially with the little bear high in the tree watching it all. I kept a lookout for Mama Bear, but she didn't appear. After a while I bade the cubs farewell and continued my hiking.

It was about sundown on Friday, June 20, when I passed through Skyland, Virginia, the upscale resort in the Shenandoah National Park. My objective for the day was Shavers Hollow Shelter, three and a half miles farther north. As I hiked by the restaurant, the wondrous smells of food cooking made me feel very hungry for a good meal. The well-dressed people at the resort looked more like wealthy tourists than outdoor enthusiasts. Sporting a bearded face and trail-worn clothing in addition to being sweaty and dirty, I decided to buy a carry-out order and take it to the lean-to to eat.

I knocked at the back door and politely asked for the manager. Explaining that I was a thru-hiker, I told him what I wanted. He informed me in no uncertain terms that they did not sell anything out the back door and slammed the door in my face. Determined to get a good meal, I walked around to the front of the restaurant and went inside.

A hush fell over the diners as I entered. I had the same feeling the good cowboy must have when he enters the saloon where the bad guys hang out. However, I was too hungry to let it bother me. I put my pack on the floor near my table and ordered a nice dinner. As I was enjoying the feast, I noticed the kitchen and wait staff kept peeping out around the doorway to see "that character out there eating."

Standing on the Appalachian Trail in the Washington Monument State Park in Maryland, I was glad to converse with another person. I would sometimes go a whole week without seeing anyone. W. Norris Weis, Director of Camp Conoy, Maryland, took this photograph in July 1951.

CHAPTER 15

Chance Meeting

After completing the Appalachian Trail in Virginia, I continued on through Maryland, spending two nights in this state. It was basically uneventful and I moved quickly on to Pennsylvania. The terrain changed about this time into an even rockier one. My feet got bruised in my lightweight shoes.

In this area I encountered an unusual sight in the deep woods highlighted by random rays of sunlight. I paused in the cool morning air to explore.

A few years before I came along, there had been a commercial airplane crash disaster. As the plane headed for the Washington, D.C., airport, it did not clear the mountain. The crash killed everyone onboard. My guidebook mentioned that the crash site was in a remote wilderness area a few yards west of the Appalachian Trail. I was curious to see if any wreckage was still there. The bodies and nearly all of the plane had been removed. Colorful wildflowers, grasses, and scrubby bushes intertwined with scraps of metal as the forest healed and reclaimed this place of hurt. I examined a few small pieces of the wrecked plane and sadly thought of all the lives that had been lost.

In later years in my profession as an aerospace engineer for the United States Air Force, I sometimes thought back on this scene. My group actually helped to design and modify planes so that they could fly very low at 500 feet to avoid enemy electronics. These planes were enabled to automatically increase altitude when encountering mountains or other obstructions. If the plane found wrecked on the

Appalachian Trail had possessed such equipment it would not have crashed. I am thankful technology has come a long way since then.

The Trail called me back and I kept hiking. On August 1, east of Swatara Gap in central Pennsylvania, I overtook a group of Boy Scouts. They invited me to accompany them down a side trail to the Bashore Scout Camp. Being an Eagle Scout myself, I felt right at home. I accepted their kind offer to spend the night. After supper in the camp mess hall, I was asked to say a few words about my hike. As I spoke, I was inspired by how engrossed the people were about my endeavor.

After the boys fell asleep, several men remained and were talking to me about my hike while their wives were talking among themselves. One was heard to say, "I've been on the Appalachian Trail – by automobile, of course." Her husband rebuked her, exclaiming, "You do not know what you are talking about!" I thought it hilarious.

On August 6, I was pleasantly surprised to meet Chester Dziengielewski at the Smith Gap Shelter in Pennsylvania. He was hiking from Maine to Georgia, so I listened eagerly as he told of his experiences. I was impressed with his efficiency and amazed at his ability to get along with the few items he carried. His cooking utensil was an old scorched coffee can that looked as if it had been in constant use since the War Between the States. Incredibly, Dziengielewski did not carry any kind of light at all on his Trail hike. As he read each page of the New Testament Bible he brought along, he would tear it out and dispose of it to save on pack weight.

Dziengielewski had not previously heard of me, and I had not heard of him. This was his second thru-hike attempt. His first was in 1950 when he started at Mount Katahdin and ended when he ran out of money at the Delaware River Gap just as he hiked into Pennsylvania. He said he went back to work in Naugatuck, Connecticut, and saved money for his current Maine to Georgia thru-hike. On this hike he was watching his spending money better.

The chance meeting proved advantageous to both of us. He told me the Trail conditions I had to face, and likewise I told him about what I had encountered. I recommended he change to long trousers instead of his shorts when he started into Virginia. Briars and thorny vines were prevalent in some of the Southern states.

Dziengielewski reached Mount Oglethorpe, Georgia, on October 10, 1951, and became the first Maine to Georgia thru-hiker and the third all-time thru-hiker. He is now deceased.

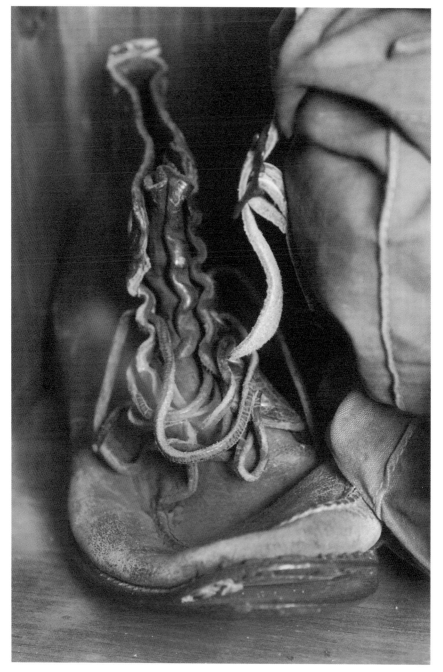

My trail-worn shoe is one from the three pairs of L.L. Bean Maine Guide shoes that served me well on my thru- hike. Although the soles wore loose from the upper parts, the bottom of the soles never wore through. Photo by Gary W. Meek.

CHAPTER 16

Misfortunes of the Soles

As I entered New Jersey on August 9, life on the Trail got a little tougher. The mosquitoes gave me a hard time as I walked. I applied oil of citronella liberally to all of my exposed flesh to try to keep them away. Big black flies also assaulted me in New Jersey and several states north. As I hiked, I would hear the buzzing of a single fly around my head. When the buzzing stopped, I knew the fly was on me preparing to bite. Smack! For miles and miles as I hiked, I would continually slap, swat and flap a dish towel around my head and neck to try to keep them away. Black flies just lavished misery on me.

My Maine guide shoes repeated the same troubling problem I had had with my first pair after the first 700 miles on the Trail. The bottom sole came loose at the toe and would catch on roots and trip me. I had to keep sewing it up with some fishing line. The second pair of my shoes sent as replacements were now wearing out.

This time I had no replacements, so I left the Trail and hiked into Port Jervis, New York, for repairs. Situated at the junction of the Neversink and Delaware rivers, the town seemed quite historic.

At a one-man shoe repair shop, I showed my shoes to the gruff-looking man busy working on a pair of men's dress shoes and explained that I needed them as I was hiking the Appalachian Trail. The repairman barely glanced up at me and growled, "I haven't got time to fool with you!" Despite my pleas, the repairman would not fix my shoes, so I had to buy a new pair from a store down the street. The new farm brogan shoes cost $12.95, so I handed the sales clerk a twenty dollar traveler's check. Only after much spirited discussion would the clerk accept my traveler's check.

In contrast, I remember trading at a small isolated store in Virginia. The one-room unpainted wooden structure had a dirt floor and no electricity. The store did not sell milk because everyone around there had their own cows. Clean and cool running water from a nearby spring flowed through a wooden trough consisting of two boards forming a V shape. The water ran from the spring into one side of a Coca-Cola box and out the other in a continuous stream, cooling the drinks inside the store. My Coca-Cola from there seemed to taste extra refreshing that day.

I enjoyed seeing this old-fashioned country store way back in the mountains. When I got ready to pay for my purchases, I handed the owner a Traveler's check. This backwoods storekeeper cashed it without batting an eye.

Years later I saw on the news that Port Jervis, New York, had been damaged by a huge flood. I turned to Eugenia and wondered aloud if the two businesses I encountered had been spared.

In 1951 the Appalachian Trail was routed on actual roads through parts of New York State. While walking on these roads, I saw property belonging to Lowell Thomas, a prominent news commentator and traveler. I passed other land owned by Thomas Dewey, who once ran for the presidency.

I temporarily wore the shoes I bought in Port Jervis until I received new L.L. Bean Maine Guide Shoes through the mail at Kent, Connecticut, on August 19. I liked these six-inch-high, lightweight L.L. Bean shoes as they didn't bind my legs or weigh me down. However, using these lightweight shoes day after day on the rocky trails of Maryland, Pennsylvania, and New Jersey hurt my feet, even though my feet were hardened and tough. The soles weren't thick enough for those rocky paths, and my feet got stone bruised.

In all, I wore out three pairs of shoes. When the stitches gave way,

I would send the shoes home and begin wearing another pair. As the heels wore down, the nails would push through inside and I would use rocks to pound them down. I had new heels put on some of my shoes, but I didn't have any of them resoled.

The continuous rough walking caused my feet to build up abnormally thick calluses on the soles. A couple of weeks after I completed my hike, these calluses peeled off. The ones that came off my heels measured about three-sixteenths of an inch thick.

One day I stopped for lunch in a very dry area. I opened a can of green string beans and began heating them over my cook stove. As I accidentally knocked over the boiler, beans spilled all over the ground. My water canteen was empty and no water was available from anywhere around. The beans had to be my lunch as there was nothing else available. I was so hungry after a long morning of hiking. In desperation I picked up each bean, put it in my mouth, removed the bean, spit out the grit, and then ate the bean. To this day I'm not too keen on string beans.

In Connecticut I went off the Trail for supplies. On my return I saw the footprints of a lone hiker. I found out later they belonged to Martin Papendick, who was hiking from Maine to Georgia. People I met would ask me about Dziengielewski and Papendick. It is mind boggling to me today when I think about how the extreme scarcity of hikers enabled me to later use information to determine exactly which hiker belonged to a single group of footprints on the Trail. What a contrast to today's vast number of hikers on the Trail!

The Trail ascended Mount Greylock, the highest peak in Massachusetts. I saw a war veteran's memorial on the summit.

While I was hiking in Massachusetts I heard a slight rustling behind me. I looked back and saw a five-foot-long black racer snake chasing a mouse. I realized they were headed right toward me! I immediately spread my legs and froze as they sped through. I observed them for several yards. As they disappeared on the Trail the chase was still on.

It added a little excitement to my hiking day. Never knowing what might suddenly happen from minute to minute was part of the fun of hiking the Appalachian Trail for me.

I later passed a Boy Scout troop camped on the Appalachian Trail. The boys were cooking breakfast, and it did smell good! I was invited to eat, but I declined. Having been a Boy Scout myself, I knew their food supply was limited, and I had already eaten my breakfast earlier. I admired a Tupperware container one of the Scouts was using. This was a plastic pitcher with the burp and seal lid that made the company famous when it was launched in 1946. He insisted I take it with me. The pitcher certainly came in handy as it was so useful in making up powdered milk.

At night I would stir the powdered milk into the water that I would get from a nearby spring. I would have to stir and stir the mixture to get it to blend before I let it set. By morning it would be ready to use. Occasionally I would put the pitcher of made-up milk in a spring to keep cool.

My Tupperware also attracted a critter. On August 30, I was sleeping on the ground in Gifford Woods State Park, Vermont. I had mixed up some milk, and the pitcher was right beside me. I woke up during the night to a sound like a cat lapping milk out of a saucer. Quietly I reached for my carbide light. When I struck the flint igniting my light, I glimpsed a big raccoon running away. The rascal had come up, tipped over this container of milk, loosened the lid, and lapped up the milk. The milk was nearly gone.

It wasn't a surprise that the raccoon could get at the milk. I was a little disappointed that I would not have the milk for the next morning's breakfast. But, I really didn't let the little things bother me.

I never had to worry about water from mountainous springs being unfit to drink. The springs consisted of cool, clear flowing water. I never had to use any purification tablets or filters in the water I drank. I carried a metal canteen of water in my backpack. Bottled water certainly was not sold in stores as it is today.

I always carried a Compak snakebite kit along with a collapsible aluminum cup in the breast pocket of my shirt. The snake-bite kit consists of a tourniquet, a razor blade to cut incisions over the fang marks, and the rubber outer part to be used to suck the venom out of the incisions. I was relieved I never had to use it.

I always used the drinking cup as an instrument to get water from a spring or stream. As a precaution I would fill the cup by dipping it down in the spring rather than getting down on my hands and knees to put my face down in the water to drink. Besides avoiding the uncomfortable position, I also prevented the possibility of being bitten in the head by a snake lurking in bushes I usually found around the edge of springs. If a snake-bite had happened like this, a tourniquet around my head would be impossible. My snake-bite kit would be useless, and so would I. Avoidance worked best for me in every way. Again, I was careful what risks I took.

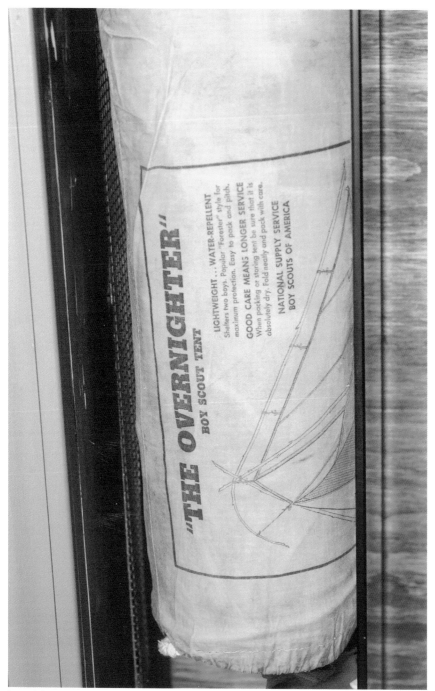

I used this Boy Scout canvas tent where there were no shelters. There was no sewn-in floor or any mosquito proof-netting. Photo by Gary W. Meek.

CHAPTER 17

Amidst the Cold and the Creatures

The Long Trail runs from Massachusetts through the Green Mountains of Vermont to Canada. The Appalachian Trail utilizes the southern portion of the Long Trail.

The summit of Stratton Mountain offered me fine views of the Green Mountains in all directions. Earl Shaffer once told me that Benton MacKaye revealed to him that he was there perched in a tall tree when he got the definite idea for the Appalachian Trail.

Leaving the Long Trail and hiking east toward New Hampshire the Appalachian Trail appeared to have been abandoned for the 18 miles to the Barnard Gulf road. I had much difficulty here as many white blazes that mark the trail were missing and much was overgrown.

By the time I got to New England, the hot, steamy summer had turned into frigid teeth-chattering fall. I began to experience ice in the mountains and fifteen-degree weather at night. I bought two suits of long winter underwear. On some nights I put on both of these in addition to my clothes before rolling up in a blanket inside my zippered sleeping bag.

While hiking on September 7 in New Hampshire through the White Mountain National Forest, I came to a side trail marked with a directional arrow and a sign: The Flume. Not knowing what a flume was and anxious not to miss anything, I took this trail. The trail turned into manmade steps with handrails, the rushing stream became faster, the scenery more spectacular. Waterfalls cascaded down the granite gorge walls. I began to see smartly dressed tourists. Finally I came to a gate and a ticket booth. I then realized that this was "the flume" and people were paying money to see it. I had entered a popular tourist attraction by the back door, so to speak. I turned and retraced my steps.

Years later I brought my wife and our two children to see this wonder. This time I entered, of course, on the paying side. I had fun telling my family the story of my original serendipitous entrance.

I enjoyed seeing God's creation evident in the peaks, viewpoints, and waterfalls. If I could go two or three miles off the Trail to see additional spectacular attractions, I'd take the side trail and have a look. Then I'd retrace my steps back and continue on the Appalachian Trail where I had departed. I kept no mileage record of these side trail hikes of which the combined mileage totaled several hundred miles.

That night a hailstorm drummed down as I stayed at Liberty Springs Shelter in the White Mountains. The next morning my heart skipped a beat when I felt a wet mass on my cheek. I wiped off the remains of a spider that was as big as the palm of my hand. I must have rolled over and crushed it during the night. I had no ill effects from the spider.

The second week in September, when I was hiking through the White Mountains, I ran into cold weather. Fortunately, the visibility was good and the scenery spectacular. Climbing the Trail in the Presidential range, I was chilled to the bone by a strong freezing wind. The Trail was a ridge walk, with continuous unobstructed views in practically every direction. As I leaned into the wind to stay on the trail, I looked longingly at a couple of homes in the valley below with smoke drifting cozily out of their fireplaces. I wondered why I was up there freezing when I could be down below, staying warm and comfortable. Only my intense determination to reach Mount Katahdin kept me going at times like this.

Twice that day I passed abandoned belts with canteens and knives. A machete was attached to one belt. Normally I would have looked over such items carefully, but on that day I was too cold to be even the least bit interested.

I sat down to rest and eat a chocolate Hershey bar, my favorite. When I finished the candy, I found that I had no desire to start walking again. I recalled reading that people had this feeling when they were freezing to death. This frightened me, and I made myself get up and start walking again. Once moving I was all right. In spite of the cold, the hike through here was worth it.

The unimpeded views throughout the White Mountains were the most spectacular and beautiful on the entire Appalachian Trail to me. The weather was cold, windy, and clear with little fog. The unique colors and shapes of the adjacent mountains blended together in varying hues. The interplay of sun and shadows over the individual mountains made for a striking show.

The white birch trees were especially breath-taking in the crisp fall air with their unusual papery textured bark and vividly colored leafy coats. I enjoyed seeing groups of them throughout the New Hampshire area. Years later on a visit to the White Mountains, our family was given some white birch logs cut in short pieces from trees on the Appalachian Trail. We valued these souvenirs, displaying them in our unused fireplace for many years.

In the White Mountains, the American Mountain Club maintains a system of huts for hikers and skiers. These are wilderness "bed and breakfasts" operated by dedicated, enthusiastic personnel. For a fee, the huts provide hot, family-style meals, trail lunches, and snacks. Beds are available for males and females. All the food and supplies have to be brought in only by backpack.

At the end of the summer when the huts were closed for the season, one room was left open for survivors. The remaining food was placed here for use by whoever needed it. I came along at a good time and was the only hiker. I used this room and the leftover food at several of their huts. My favorite find was several large containers of different flavors of preserves and loaves of bread.

On September 11, at my last hut, the Carter Notch Hut, I met Joseph B. Dodge. As the manager of all the American Mountain Club huts, he and several others were in the process of closing it for the cold season. They were exceptionally accommodating to me. When it came time to bed down, Dodge told me if I slept on a bed in the main room he would have to charge me a fee. Or I could sleep on the floor in another area for free. The floor worked out fine for me. I was just glad to be out of the cold wind and in a warm place.

When I went off the Trail on September 12 to a store in Gorham, New Hampshire, a woman news reporter warned me that on several occasions a big black panther had been seen in the section I was about to enter. I was polite to her but inwardly I shrugged off the warning just as I had the many warnings about rattlesnakes that I had received along the way. These people were most sincere with their warnings, but their fears were unfounded for the most part. I knew to use caution in a reasonable way.

The first night after leaving Gorham I made camp at the Trident lean-to. When I retired for the night, I extinguished my light and sat in my sleeping bag for a few minutes as I usually did, listening to the sounds of wildlife out in the darkness. It was always interesting to try to identify the different sounds' origins.

In the moonlight I saw a shadowy animal coming up the trail. My breath was coming pretty fast as I tried to determine if it was the panther. Was the reporter right about *the* panther? I picked up a short section of a small log and hurled it toward the animal. Before that piece landed, I had another piece in the air. The first chunk narrowly missed the animal, and as it ran away, I could see that it was just a big porcupine. This was not the first porcupine I had seen on the Trail or the last.

As I hiked north from Trident lean-to, I saw and admired a steep rock cliff in the distance. I was surprised to find that the Trail led to the base of this cliff, which was called Wocket Ledge. I started climbing. Partway up, a rock handhold broke away and I started sliding. At the foot of the steep slope, I fell over a small cliff. I landed in a heap, upside down on the top of my pack. I remained in a curled-up position, with my head tucked down, until the loose rocks and sand quit falling on me from the slope above.

The first thing I did was to listen to my watch to see if it was still ticking. Once again my sturdy watch came through for me. Then I checked my arms and legs to see if they were okay. My left arm was bloody, but the injury was not serious. I was more frightened than physically hurt. I quietly realized I could have been injured to the point of being flat on my back until someone came along to help, whenever that would be.

I had lost confidence in my ability to climb straight up over this ledge so I went to the side of the trail where I could use trees as aids in climbing. This time I was successful in reaching the top. When I came to a stream and washed the sand out of my clothes and the blood off my arm, I was practically as good as new. I was so thankful that I was not seriously hurt and that I could continue my hike.

By the time I reached Maine, I really had a beard! Due to the rarity of beards, I was sometimes addressed as "Rip" or "Moses." Passing a group of hikers, I heard them comment on how spry I was for my age. This was only the first occurrence of this type of comment. It added some humor to my day.

Just after I crossed into Maine, I followed two bobcats for several minutes. I was within thirty yards of them when one bobcat looked back. As soon as he saw me, both animals disappeared.

I noticed porcupines several times. On one occasion I glanced up to find myself eyeball to eyeball with a porcupine in a tree. It looked like an overstuffed house cat with hundreds of sharp quills.

About sundown on September 17, the day I left Grafton Notch, Maine, I found a cabin with a sign that read "Ten Of Clubs." The door had obviously been ajar for some time and the porcupines had left their "evidence." The fact that the intruders had been porcupines was obvious to my nose as I had smelled the same odor sometimes emitting from porcupines on the Trail. I cleaned up the cabin, cooked supper, and spread my sleeping bag over the bunk mattress I had flipped over. Before retiring, I barricaded the door.

During the night, I was awakened by the sound of an animal chewing. I got up and, with a candle that was found in the cabin in one hand and my stick in the other, investigated the noises. In a corner I found a big porcupine chewing on a wooden cupboard. I didn't want him for a roommate, so I nudged him with my stick, then stepped back to allow him to escape. He scampered across the floor and went out through a hole in the wall. I plugged up the hole with firewood and went back to sleep.

In the southern Maine wilderness, I met a bear hunter carrying a high-powered rifle and a bucket of bread scraps. He was checking bear traps he had previously set out around the area. I asked him how big the bears were in those parts. He said the largest he knew of weighed about 750 pounds. Somehow after seeing him I was more afraid of stepping in a bear trap in these desolate woods than I was of the bears themselves. I saw no bears in Maine, or bear traps fortunately.

In a thickly wooded area in Maine, I heard something big like a moose make a loud splashing noise as it exited a nearby pond. Through the thicket, I could see disturbed water in the part of the pond visible to me. I focused my eyes on a clearing where I guessed the moose would pass, but I did not see anything. I did see moose tracks often on the Appalachian Trail in Maine and was quite disappointed that I never saw a moose.

When I was ascending the Bigelow Range Trail in Maine, I heard the sound of thundering hooves. I quickly moved to one side as two huge horses came down the trail. These horses were twice as big as any horse I'd ever seen. I gave them plenty of room. They were harnessed side by side and dragging a heavy log between them. There was no teamster. The horses had been trained to move logs from the cutting area to a loading site down the mountain by themselves. This was an impressive sight.

In southern Maine, I ascended a mountain with a metal fire tower on its summit. I enjoyed a fine panoramic view from the base of the tower, so I didn't feel the need to climb it. It did not appear to be manned. As I walked closely by one of the metal supports to the tower, I hit the support with my hiking staff. WHA-A-AM! I don't know why I did it. I guess I just wanted to hear the metallic noise out in the remote woods. To my great surprise there was an observer in the tower! I had just scared the daylights out of him. He was in shock as he jerked open the bottom entrance door. I apologized profusely, but what was done was done. I continued my hike secure in the knowledge that this was the extent of my "mischief" on the Appalachian Trail.

When I first saw the Kennebec River in Maine, I thought I might have some trouble crossing it because of its swift current and floating pulpwood logs. There was no bridge; only two small boats sat, one on each side of the river. I decided it looked like a good plan to me. I was experienced with boats, so I unhesitatingly climbed into the boat on my side of the river. I picked up the long metal-tipped pole I found, headed the boat toward a point upstream on the far bank and poled off.

Before I could make a second stroke with my pole, the boat was about twenty yards downstream. My confidence left me in the fast-moving water. The logs being floated downstream to a paper mill began ramming the boat. I used my pole again. The water was only about five feet deep, but the current was very swift. By poling furiously, I finally reached the opposite shore about fifty yards downstream. I jumped into the water and pulled the boat back upstream to the point where the other boat was tied. I left my backpack and staff on the river bank. Fortunately, they did not get wet.

Now my problem was to tie the boats together and pole across the stream again in order to leave the first boat where I found it. I accomplished this second crossing with much less difficulty. Finally, the third crossing was made and I was safely across the Kennebec River with each boat in its proper place, ready for the next traveler.

I never would have thought I'd need my previously obtained skills with boats to hike on the Appalachian Trail, but it really paid off at this time. Today, there is a boat and operator available to carry hikers across the Kennebec River during certain hours.

CHAPTER 18

Summit Day at Last

On the final day of my incredible thru-hike adventure, I hiked from the Rainbow Lake lean-to, reaching Katahdin Stream Campground in the afternoon. Ice and snow lay in the shadows, reminding me of the cold, but I barely felt the chill. My excitement was running high, and I felt like my feet were getting lighter somehow. My goal once so distant was now just right in front of my eyes!

I took this photograph at "The End of the Trail" on Mount Katahdin, Maine, on September 30, 1951. My trusty hiking staff leans against the sign amid the snow in the shadows of the rocks.

When I arrived at Katahdin Stream Campground, I was given a fine welcome by the Baxter State Park Ranger Fred Pittman and his wife. He had been alerted and was watching for me. I thankfully left

My smile shows my joy and exhilaration as I stood at the Katahdin Stream Campground on September 30, 1951. I had just descended Mount Katahdin, reaching the completion of my thru-hike of 123 days.

my heavy pack at their cabin. I climbed Mount Katahdin with only my loyal hiking stick, relishing the glorious feeling of conquest. I reached the summit of Mount Katahdin at 4:35 p.m., thus completing this journey that had been such a greatly anticipated goal. From every aspect it was a beautiful day on September 30, 1951.

From the summit of Mount Katahdin the visibility was excellent and the scenery was spectacular in all directions. It was an emotional experience. When I reached the sign marking the northern terminus of the Appalachian Trail, I knelt down and said a prayer of thanks to God for watching over me and allowing me to make the hike. It had been one of the highlights of my life.

The realization that I had actually hiked the 2,000-plus miles, culminating in the fulfillment of my dream, took a while to sink in. The combination of my upbringing, outdoor experiences, creativity, and faith in God had brought me to this high point. The process had strengthened me in so many ways. My planning and determination had paid off even with so much unknown that had been before me. Life was good!

I hiked quickly down the mountain and returned to the ranger's cabin at the Katahdin Stream Campground just before dark. I had a tiny audience with which to share my big news of triumph. Other than the Pittmans, there was no one else at the campground. I saw no hikers on either my hike up Mount Katahdin or the return. I spent the night at the Katahdin Stream campground.

Little did I know then that I would have the many, many opportunities to tell my Trail stories, as I have for the rest of my life. I didn't know people would become so interested in the Appalachian Trail, but I did understand that it could provide many opportunities for wondrous experiences.

I visited with Ranger Fred Pitman at the office of Baxter State Park on September 30, 1951. Ranger Pitman enjoyed hearing Trail stories and looking over my hiking equipment displayed on the table.

PAGE FOUR

The Lewiston Daily Sun

Saturday, October 6, 1951

Up the Appalachian Trial

While most everyone else has been fretting about high taxes, inflation, the war in Korea and the Giants' race for the National League pennant, a young man has been spending the summer plodding northward over the Appalachian Trail from Georgia to Mt. Katahdin.

A few days ago he arrived at Millinocket, after reaching the summit of Maine's highest mountain. In the space of 123 days he walked 2,025 miles, wore out three pairs of shoes, killed 15 rattlesnakes with his walking-stick, grew a long beard, and lost 28 pounds. He was only the second man in history to cover the full length of the trail, which winds from Mt. Oglethorpe northward over hundreds of other summits to central Maine.

To those who have no fondness for mountains or for mountain climbing, this adventure may have seemed merely another way to spend the summer months, and not a very good way at that. To those acquainted with the Trail, it is a feat of great endurance that stamps the young Georgian as a man of fortitude and courage.

We wonder what he thought when passing over the Presidential Range, with its unmatched scenery, or picking his way carefully through Mahoosuc Notch, or down the sheer side of Mt. Spec, in Oxford county. He has seen what few people are ever privileged to see; he has conquered the most exacting thoroughfare found in this country, at least. We take off our hat to Eugene M. Espy, of Cordele, Georgia. The young man set his sights on a distant goal, and reached it, and who can say there isn't something worthy in that?

This editorial praising my "feat of endurance" was written by the *Lewiston Daily Sun* of Lewiston, Maine.

CHAPTER 19

A Royal Reception

Upon my return to the Katahdin Stream campground, Ranger Pittman called Millinocket, Maine, and the following day a newspaper reporter, Mrs. Chase, and a photographer, Mr. Crowell, drove out to see me. I later learned from Mrs. Chase that she and Crowell had met Earl Shaffer at the same campground when he finished the Appalachian Trail in 1948. Mrs. Chase interviewed him, and Crowell took his picture for the Associated Press.

At Katahdin Stream Campground, I had noticed a semi-tame deer that seemed to have a special interest in the campground. While waiting on the "press corps," I was disposing of trail food that I wouldn't need any longer when I saw the deer standing a short distance away. I filled my hand with sugar and raisins and slowly extended it toward the deer, remaining as motionless as possible. Curiosity won out. The deer cautiously walked closer and closer, perhaps hoping that I had some food for him. After spying my tasty snack, he hastily ate all the food right out of my hand. He turned and retreated to the edge of the clearing.

Later Mrs. Chase and Mr. Crowell arrived from Millinocket. The photographer positioned me for a picture with Mount Katahdin in the background. While he was adjusting his camera, I spied the same deer watching us. I held out my hand as if I had more food. This time he came right over and licked the palm of my hand, stepped back, disappointed at finding no more food. The deer jerked up its head and leaped away, and I saw his tail waving goodbye as he disappeared into the woods.

We later realized that in the split second of interaction, the quick-thinking photographer Crowell had snapped this scene just in time to produce an amazing picture! I have enjoyed showing this photograph and saying that on my hike I lived in the wilds so long that this deer thought I was just another deer.

Later a local artist painted a large oil painting of this photograph for me. It hangs prominently over my hiking stick on the wall of our family room as a wonderful reminder of a grand goal achieved.

Mrs. Chase wrote a lengthy article about me that headlined one of the sections of the *Bangor Daily News*. Featuring four nice pictures, it was a well-written article about my hike and me. I was most appreciative.

The article contained a tidbit that was somewhat humorous to me. Mrs. Chase had asked me how much weight I lost. I told her I did not know. I did lose weight but I also gained muscle mass. She asked, "How much did you weigh when you started your hike?" When I told her, she said, "Well, you certainly don't weigh that much now." The next day I read her article about me in the *Bangor Daily News* and saw where I had lost 28 pounds.

While in Millinocket, I did not phone my parents to announce that I had reached Mount Katahdin. My family never made long-distance telephone calls unless it was an emergency. I had not made any calls during my hike, and I did not think completion of my hike qualified as an emergency. I mailed them a one-cent postcard to tell them the news.

I did not know that anything concerning my hike had been picked up by the Associated Press. The AP sent my captioned picture throughout the United States. A neighbor in Cordele heard about me on a radio news broadcast and immediately called my parents. My parents received this message before they received my card. I was dating my future wife at the time. Eugenia read it in an Atlanta newspaper. Clearly, the communication about such things is vastly different today with cell phones, internet and e-mail.

When I met the president of the local Chamber of Commerce in Millinocket, he invited me to speak at a banquet that would take place in a couple of days. He said I was not scheduled to be there, of course, but they wanted to hear about my hike. I was to keep my beard, wear my trail clothes, and talk for twenty minutes. I accepted his invitation, having no idea that this was just the first of many speeches I would give throughout my life sharing what I had thought was a private adventure.

The president of the Chamber of Commerce was the manager of a nearby Great Northern paper mill. At his invitation, I was guest for a day at his mill. The process of making paper from logs was most interesting. I enjoyed seeing how logs such as the ones I had encountered in the Kennebec River were processed. The tour helped transition me from my placid world of wilderness into the always intriguing world of industry, awakening thoughts of my industrial management education at Georgia Tech.

Mrs. Chase generously offered for me to stay in her home while I was in Millinocket. I enjoyed being a guest in her nice, spacious home and swapping stories with her. I ate some of my meals out in restaurants, where I garnered a lot of attention due to my appearance.

I got amused while I was in the Millinocket Post Office mailing some cards. I had kept my hiking appearance as requested for my talk. I saw two ladies looking me over as they walked toward the exit. I overheard one say to the other, "That certainly is a spry old man!"

From my long beard, people in Millinocket began to recognize me and really give me the royal treatment. I got invited to meals and for visits in people's homes. I accepted a lunch invitation from a Maine guide who owned a camp that was on the Appalachian Trail. He had already closed the camp up for the winter when I hiked by it. The store where I bought a suit of "Sunday clothes" gave me a big discount. The very outdoor-minded Maine citizens showed much enthusiasm for my accomplishment.

The next day after speaking to the Chamber of Commerce, I sent my pack and staff to Georgia by railway express. I then visited a barber shop to get a much-needed haircut and shave. I put on my new clothes and hitchhiked the five hundred miles to Boston making good time. It was a late Friday afternoon when I got on the highway to try to catch a ride to New York City. I met lots of uniformed sailors also hitchhiking. Knowing that motorists would pick up the military before civilians, I flagged down a Greyhound bus headed for New York City. I used bus service all the way to Georgia, relishing in the luxury of sitting down while moving.

During my long bus ride, I tallied up what I had spent achieving my dream. I spent $400 total: $300 for my equipment, hiking clothes, and food, plus $100 for bus fare and new clothes for the trip back to Georgia. Today, such a thru-hike obviously would cost a great deal more.

On my thru-hike I wore out three pairs of shoes, three pairs of pants, and two shirts. The nylon socks were still wearable since they didn't have a single hole in them. Grass stains acquired through the many miles of walking outdoors had dyed the socks a dull green. My equipment was still in good shape. The star of my equipment, my hiking stick, had proved to be a very sturdy asset along the Trail.

My arrival home in Cordele was rather anti-climactic. My parents were happy to see me. They said they were glad I didn't get hurt. Otherwise, it was business as usual at the Espy household. I realized that they did not really comprehend the magnitude of the feat I had just accomplished nor the risks involved. I had largely kept the potential dangers to myself to avoid worry on their part. Most of the other people in Cordele didn't seem to understand about my thru-hike, either, although they were very kind with their comments. In those pre-television days, people were not as interested in other parts of the country, particularly regarding outdoor activities.

Throughout my hike I corresponded regularly with Eugenia every three or four hundred miles. Staying in touch with these letters meant so much to both of us. It was exciting to see each other again after my long journey. Among Eugenia's first words to me were, "I never had any doubt that you wouldn't make it all the way!" I had felt her support the entire time. She was eager to hear all about it, and I enjoyed sharing my stories with her.

I was tenth to hike the entire Appalachian Trail and the second thru-hiker. My 123-day hike started May 31, 1951, and ended September 30, 1951. When I began my thru-hike, I had not heard of the Georgia Appalachian Trail, or either Shaffer or Avery. I just wanted to experience the hike and thought it sounded like a lot of fun. My desire to hike every foot of the Trail has caused some people to think of me as a purist.

My hike gave me much satisfaction, enjoyment, and appreciation for the beauty of the Appalachian Mountains. After its completion, however, I had no desire to hike back to Georgia. I experienced no readjustment period when I returned home – it was "business as usual." I relaxed, and enjoyed seeing friends and family. The comforts and conveniences of home life were appreciated more.

Shortly after returning to Georgia, I met Andrew Sparks, longtime editor of the *Atlanta Journal and Constitution* Sunday magazine section. He was excited about my hike and wanted to write a feature article. We rode to Mount Oglethorpe together with his photographer. Sparks devoted a lot of time to write a superb article.

The following is an excerpt published in the book, *Friendships of the Trail*, by the Georgia Appalachian Trail Club in 1981.

"An October 1951 GATC bulletin reported the following:

Report on the 2050 Mile Club: This past weekend, the Georgia Appalachian Trail Club really hit the jack-pot! After the embarrassing experience of having a Georgia boy from Georgia Tech (our own personal stamping ground) complete the entire Appalachian Trail without any of us ever having heard of him, we fell heir to a couple of young fellows from the North who had just come in from Mt. Katahdin, one having completed non-stop the entire 2050 miles of the Appalachian Trail and the other having covered all except 300 miles which he bypassed by bus.

There has already been some publicity in the papers and magazines regarding the exploits of the Georgia boy, Eugene Espy of Cordele, Georgia. The other two are Chester Dziengielewski (pronounced DINGLEWESKI) of Naugatuck, Connecticut (age 27) and Bill Hall of East Liverpool, Ohio (age 19). They arrived together at Mt. Oglethorpe on October 10, and came down to Jasper where they chanced to meet Andy Sparks of The Atlanta Journal staff who was at Jasper getting some additional information for a story on Eugene Espy. Mr. Sparks brought the boys back to Atlanta with him and put them in touch with the Georgia Appalachian Trail Club. They were invited out to Jim Proctor's home where they stayed until Sunday. Arrangements were made for them to have a telephone call to their homes and also to call Eugene Espy at Cordele, whom they had passed on the Trail. They were also taken to Sears Roebuck where each purchased a new outfit of clothing as theirs were in a sad shape from the standpoint of wear and tear.

Mr. Sparks had already interviewed them for a feature story in the Sunday Magazine section (a combined story about all three boys will be in an early issue); and on Saturday morning, he arranged for them to make a transcription of about 15 minutes "question and answer" program which was broadcast over WSB that afternoon.

On Saturday afternoon, Eugene Espy came up to Atlanta and had a reunion with the boys at Jim Proctor's and the three, with Jim acting as interviewer, made a one hour tape recording of their experiences and impressions while on the Trail. As a matter of interest, Earl Shaffer, who was the first person to complete the entire 2050 miles of the Trail in one continuous hike, knew about at least one of the boys and made a short trip along the Trail with him in one of the Northern States .... We have invited all three boys to go up to the Smokies with us this next weekend for the trip to Ramsay Cascade and to meet Mr. Benton MacKaye. They have all accepted."

The weekend trip we took was to the "Cabin in the Briar" in Tennessee where the GATC and other hiking clubs were meeting for fellowship. We enjoyed swapping stories and answering lots of questions from the other hikers. Benton MacKaye met the group for dinner in Gatlinburg. I felt so honored to meet him and was pleased that the admiration was mutual. Upon his return home, MacKaye wrote to Marene Snow of the GATC, thanking her and the Club for the occasion:

"At last I have a moment to send you some word of my existence, and the merry life I've led since you got me started on it, at that (for me) superlative occasion with the GATC folks. Not since Cloudland, in '34, have I had such an experience. Indeed, it marked a new era in itself. To sit there with three men who actually walked a path of fantasy gave me a sense of reality which I never expected to obtain. It gave me a sort of "destination feeling," a reaching of the end of a thirty-year journey. Nothing that could be done for me, in the length of the whole AT, could have more deeply touched me than what you and your vital little band did for me that night. Please give each my special and affectionate sentiments .... (November 7, 1951) "

Other publicity immediately after my hike included:

Associated Press (Newspapers and radio all over the U.S.)

Bangor Daily News (Maine)

The Lewiston Daily Sun (Maine)

Field and Stream Magazine

Quick Magazine

Macon Telegraph (Georgia)

Cordele Dispatch (Georgia)

Strangers from all over the U.S. mailed me clippings of the Associated Press article and picture appearing in their hometown newspapers. I was quite touched by the response.

The increased publicity about the Appalachian Trail produced more public awareness of its existence and the need for preserving such natural lands. More people became curious, went on day hikes, and got hooked on hiking.

About half of the Appalachian Trail in 1951 was on private land or public roads. The private land owners gave permission for the Trail to go through their property. Occasionally, the owners would become dissatisfied and withdraw their permission. This would necessitate relocation of the Trail. These owners might have suffered financially due to hikers damaging fences, stiles, or failing to close gates. As the number of hikers grew, the problems increased.

In 1951, in addition to the various hiking clubs maintaining the Trail, there were less than 300 individual members of the Appalachian Trail Conference. In contrast, now there are about 40,000 members of the renamed Appalachian Trail Conservancy and nearly all the Trail is government owned.

Few people hiked in 1951. Several times I went an entire week without seeing anyone. The Appalachian Trail was not as well-known back then as it is now. Those living close by called it the "Government Trail." When I hiked, I came across fewer trail shelters and road crossings. There were American Mountain Club huts in the White Mountains, but no hiker hostels anywhere on the Trail. Hostels today play a large part in hiker culture along the Appalachian Trail.

The current 2,175 mile Appalachian Trail, with its many improvements since 1951, is well-maintained and easy to follow. Climbing and stepping over blowdowns has been eliminated. Bushwhacking is rarely needed. Most road walking has been relocated to the wilderness. Steps, ladders, metal rungs, bridges, boardwalks, and shelters have been added. It is still a strenuous and difficult Trail.

MR. JOHN DENT BURNETT

ROUTE 1

IVANHOE, VIRGINIA
January 2, 1952

Dear Mr. Espy,

Thank you for your letter and the clippings. We all enjoyed reading them and we are so glad you remember us and have been so thoughtful about sending us cards and otherwise remembering us. Thank you too for the Christmas card.

I am going to send you the clipping which came out in the Galax Gazette when you were here and again when the other "hiker" came through. You will enjoy them more than we would since you did not get one and I doubt that one is available at this date. As you will see we have had them in our scrap book.

J.D. Jr. is not yet an Eagle. A very severe polio epidemic prevented his getting his Life Saving Merit badge but he will have it this summer we hope.

We are sorry the dog disturbed you the night you were sleeping out here but I daresay you will remember that longer than you would have one night that you had no such an experience. Perhpas you would not have remembered us at all otherwise. We no longer have Tip but have a little blonde cocker Spaniel house dog.

We hope you have as successful on which ever venture you undertake next- the Missippi or the sea of matrimony. Wonder which is the most adventurous?

Your parents must be very glad to have you home from so many wanderings. And You must have quite an entertaining list of adventures.

When you come back to Virginia stop to see us.

The very best of every thing for the new year.

Most cordially yours,

J. D. Burnetts

I received this letter from J.D. Burnett of Ivanhoe, Virginia. I stayed on the Trail with several families like the Burnetts who showed interest in my adventure.

"IN THE SHADOW OF MT. LECONTE"   — MOUNTAIN VIEW HOTEL —   GATLINBURG, TENNESSEE

Benton MacKaye,
Shirley Center, Mass.
Tel,
    C/o Harry Johnson,
        Shirley 502

    C/o Wilderness Society,
    1840 Mintwood Place N.W.,
    Washington 9, D. C.
    COlumbia 1588
        Howard Zahniser,
            Exec Sec'y

Autograph of Benton Mackaye, November 7, 1951.

List of Overnight Stopping Places

Gene Espy's Thru-Hike 1951

GEORGIA

May

  31 Spring near Southern's Store

June

    1 Porch of Frosty Mountain Cabin

    2 Hawk Mountain Fire Tower

    3 Woody Gap picnic table

    4 Tesnatee Gap Lean-to

    5 Rocky Knob Lean- to

    6 Snake Mountain Shelter

    7 Hoke Eller's attic

NORTH CAROLINA – TENNESSEE

    8 Deep Gap Lean-to

    9 Deep Gap Lean-to

  10 White Oak Bottoms Lean-to

  11 Wayah Gap Lean-to

  12 Wesser Creek Lean-to

  13 Cable Gap Lean-to

  14 Fontana Village Lodge

  15 Spence Field Lean-to

  16 Silers Bald Lean-to

  17 Little Indian Gap Lean-to

  18 Hughes Ridge Lean-to

  19 Waterville School

20 Walnut Mountain Lean-to

21 Hot Springs, North Carolina

22 Spring Mountain Lean-to

23 Locust Ridge Lean-to

24 Hayloft at Spivey Gap

25 Curley Maple Gap Lean-to

26 Blue Springs School

27 F.R. Scott

VIRGINIA

28 Damascus, jail

29 Skulls Gap

30 Comers Rock

July

1 Byllesby Station

2 F. Paul Bronnock

3 Fancy Gap Store

4 John R. Barnard

5 Hayloft at Rock Castle

6 Emmett Pate's old store

7 Poor Mountain

8 Porch at Mason Cove

9 G.L. Crawford's barn

10 Bearwallow Gap

11 Natural Bridge Station

12 Snowden

13 Rocky Row Run

14 Brown Mountain Café

15 Rocky Mountain Fire Tower

16 Reeds Gap

17 Sawmill Run Shelter

18 Pinefield Shelter

19 South River Shelter

20 Shavers Hollow Shelter

21 Elk Wallow Shelter

22 Mosby Shelter

23 Mrs. O.T. Adams, Paris

24 Wilson Gap Shelter

MARYLAND

25 Rocky Run Shelter

26 Devils Racecourse Shelter

PENNSYLVANIA

27 Quarry Gap Shelter

28 Tagg Run Shelter

29 Harrisburg, YMCA

30 Harrisburg, YMCA

31 Mt. Laurel churchyard

August

1 Bashore Scout Camp

2 Hertlein Lean-to

3 Port Clinton

4 Allentown Shelter

5 Mountain near Lehigh Gap

6 Smith Gap Lean-to

7 Religious retreat building

8 Portland

NEW JERSEY – NEW YORK

9 Catfish Fire Tower

10 High Point Lean-to No.2

11 High Point Lean-to No.1

12 Vernon, New Jersey

13 New Jersey – New York line

14 Three miles beyond Mount Peter

15 Bear Mountain Lake

16 Indian Pond

17 Torrey Memorial Lean-to

18 Webatuck Lean-to

CONNECTICUT

19 Mountain near Kent

20 Chase Mountain Lean-to

21 Pine Knoll Lean-to

MASSACHUSETTS

22 Sages Ravine

23 Mt. Wilcox Lean-to

24 October Mountain Lean-to

25 Kitchen Brook Lean-to

VERMONT

26 Thendara Shelter

27 Webster Shelter

28 Mad Tom Shelter

29 Greenwall Shelter

30 Gifford Woods State Park

31 Woodstock

NEW HAMPSHIRE

September

1 Dartmouth Outing Club Office

2 Dartmouth Outing Club Office

3 Mt. Cube Lean-to

4 Porch of Great Bear Cabin

5 Mt. Kinsman

6 Kinsman Pond Shelter

7 Liberty Spring Shelter

8 Galehead Hut

9 Saco River Bridge

10 Madison Spring Hut

11 Carter Notch Hut

12 Gorham

13 Trident Lean-to

MAINE

14 Full Goose Shelter

15 Full Goose Shelter

16 Old Speck warden's cabin

17 Ten of Clubs Cabin

18 Sabbath Day Pond Lean-to

19 Poplar Ridge Lean-to

20 Horns Pond Lean-to

21 Jerome Brook Lean-to

22 Caratunk

23 Caratunk

24 Emma Willer, Monson

25 Emma Willer, Monson

26 West Chairback Pond

27 White Cap ranger's cabin

28 Antlers Camp

29 Rainbow Lake Lean-to

30 Katahdin Stream Campground

I am in front of the Appalachian Trail exhibit in the Visitors Center at Amicalola Falls State Park, Georgia. Much of my hiking gear is featured in the display case. Photo by Gary W. Meek.

UNIT III

CHAPTER 20
Trail Afterthoughts

I hiked quietly and enjoyed the solitude of the Appalachian Trail. The wildlife I encountered included eight black bears, several hundred whitetail deer, cottontail rabbits, both red and gray squirrels, flying squirrels, opossums, porcupines, red foxes, raccoons, skunks, chipmunks, bobcats, mice, rats, turtles, American toads, frogs, lizards, timber rattlesnakes, copperhead snakes, and birds such as ruffed grouses, killdeers, bobwhites, whip-poor-wills, pileated woodpeckers, great horned owls, screech owls, bald eagles, blue jays, brown thrashers, chickadees, cardinals, and Canadian geese.

A couple of times where the Trail went through a large pasture I found cows living in the hiking shelters. Hikers in today's shelters are annoyed by lots of mice. The shelters I used had few if any mice. The increase of hikers carrying food brought the mice.

In a few places in the South, the Trail had eroded into a small ditch. Birds' nests were frequently built among the exposed tree roots. I was, as always, careful where I stepped. I enjoyed hearing the excited little chirps and seeing two or three cute baby birds with their mouths wide open awaiting food from their parents.

Ruffed grouse build their nests on the ground. In the South, occasionally as I approached a nest, the grouse hen fluttered across the Trail, one wing dragging on the ground like it was broken. She had hushed her chicks and darted out to lure me away with her wounded bird act.

Several times I had to hike around small lakes made by beavers damming a stream. In a few cases, I was able to see the beavers themselves.

I more often saw evidence of their teeth marks on stumps.

Animals were sometimes in my path on the Trail, although I'm sure they looked at me as the one in the way. Twice I came up on deer bedded down for the night right on the Trail – until they heard and saw me. One day I nearly stepped on a pair of foxes that I did not see bedded down in the ground growth. When I startled them, they scared me by jumping up and running away. Other times I saw foxes that were farther away, scooting through the underbrush.

At times I fell asleep while listening to the screech of a nearby owl among the other "members of the symphony." Sometimes I could glimpse an owl flying illuminated by moonlight on its nightly patrol.

My time in the wilderness helped me to really appreciate the incredible ways the different animals live their lives and try to survive. Hikers today probably do not see as much wildlife as I did. Although I am glad more people are hiking the Appalachian Trail today, the sounds and sight of so many more hikers keep more of the animals away from being seen on the Trail itself. For me, seeing glimpses of animals made my hike interesting and unpredictable every day.

One of the drawbacks to hiking alone is not being able to share the delight of sightings of animals, plants, trees, beautiful scenery, and sometimes gorgeous sunsets with another person. I developed a great appreciation for these things and kept their images in my heart as best I could. Later on as a husband, father, and grandfather, I have passed my joy of discovery of such things on to my family. Pointing out sights such as a hummingbird or a pretty sky to each other just makes our day more special.

* * *

When I wrote the Appalachian Trail Conference about my thru-hiking plans in 1951, I received a most helpful reply from Jean Stephenson. A Trail worker since 1932, she was the founder of the original *Appalachian Trailway News*, former editor-in-chief of all Conference publications, and a member of the Board of Managers for fourteen years. She loaned me her south to north pages from several of the guidebooks and asked me to note any changes needed.

Fontana Dam, N.C.
October 31, 1951

Dear Mr. Espy:

I was pleased to get your cards and to know that you completed the hike of the entire Applachian trail. I must confess that I figured you would give it up before finishing it.

Some few days back a young man stopped here who was headed toward Georgia, having completed the hike from Maine. I am sorry that I do not have his name, however, I did not meet him myself.

I guess you got a big reception when you returned home. You know that must of been quite an experience making it by yourself.

If you are ever in this locality again please stop by and see us.

Best of regards,

Frank W. Smiley, Lt.
Public Safety Service

SIGHTS AND SOUNDS IN FONTANA

A better man than most is red-bearded Eugene M. Espy, of Cordele, Ga., who stopped over here last night.

Loaded down with a back-pack, Gene is hiking the Appalachian Trail north from Mt Oglethorpe, Ga. He's already arranged for shoe replacements.

Fontana Village Newsletter.

December 29, 1952

Mr. Eugene M. Espy
Cordele, Georgia

        Your Christmas card of Dec. 22 gave me much pleasure. And your reply to my letter of last January was a help to me. Your article in the Appalachian Trailway News of Jan. 1952 I read carefully three or four times and learned much from it. North of Sherburne Pass in Vt. I missed the Trail just as you did. A man living near there said that he understood that there had been no trail there for 15 years. I also talked with Prof. Buckhanon(sp.?) who was working that section. I got about 10 miles north of Sherburne Pass then found no blazes and no trail and went around to where the Trail runs into a little road. So I missed about 2 miles of Trail there.

        In Mahoosuc Pass where you had a bad fall, I sprained my left knee in the middle of the morning, but not bad enough to stop me. The next morning I had to drag the stiff knee for a mile or more before I could bend it much, just as I had expected. It caused me very little trouble, but did not recover entirely until I was home for weeks.

        But my experience with snakes was very different from yours, perhaps because I started much earlier in the season. I didn't see one poisonous snake, so far as I know.

        Every day I made out a sheet like the enclosed. I ran off plenty of them on the mimeograph so I have more copies than I need. Just throw this one away when you are thru with it. I wrote a long article on my walk for the Trailway News, but I don't know how much of it Jean will print. The Potomac Club Bulletin (to be out in Feb. I am told) will also have some account of my trip.

        I was aiming at finishing in about 120 days and reached the halfway post in 60.5 days, then took 78.5 days to walk the second half. It rained on 64 of the 139 days, and I was sick at Long Trail Lodge for 3 or 4 days and for 4 days before I got to that Lodge. At Brumley lodge (a big frame shelter enclosed on all sides) I found some potatoes, an onion, and pancake syrup. I cooked the pots and onion and ate the stuff. There was also some rolled oats. That night I had pains inside and the next day diarrhea. But for two days I still made the regular distance – about 20 miles. Then the night of the second day I got worse and the third day I went only about 7 miles (over Killington Mtn.) and stayed at Pico Shelter. The next morning I dragged myself thru the drizzle to Long Trail Lodge. The people there were wonderfully kind and generous. They could not have done more for me if I had been their own grandmother.

        You certainly made a hit with the people along the Trail. I saw dozens of them that remembered you pleasantly and praised you in various ways, beginning with the Caldwells at Suches and all the way to Mrs. Chase and the Chamber of Commerce in Millinocket. And in between those two many people pointed out where you slept and told about your pack and equipment, what you told them, etc.

        The Trail was very good in places, but on the whole it was far worse than I had expected and in places there simply was NO trail. But I am glad that I had the experience and hope to see you sometime to talk about it.
                         Gratefully,

                         George F. Miller

In this letter George F. Miller who hiked the Trail in 1952 confirmed the deplorable conditions on some parts of the Trail that I encountered on my thru-hike in 1951. In the last paragraph, Mr. Miller wrote about the favorable comments from people I met along my hike.

One guide correctly specified crossing Fontana Dam; however, at the end, when the hiker comes to a road, the directions incorrectly stated to turn left. I followed the road until I ran into the old abandoned trail leading from Deals Gap to Shuckstack Mountain. I bushwhacked on this trail until it ran into the 1946-47 relocated Trail to Shuckstack Ridge; I corrected this problem in the guide pages I carried.

It was a pleasure to meet Jean Stephenson at the Twelfth Appalachian Trail Conference at Skyland Lodge in the Shenandoah National Park. She put so much energy and dedication into making sure others could enjoy the Appalachian Trail.

* * *

In the mid 1970s Rodale Press, Inc., contacted some of the early hikers of the entire Appalachian Trail. Mr. James R. Hare was editing a book, *Hiking the Appalachian Trail*, for Rodale. Each of these hikers was to write and send him the story of their hike. Each would be a separate chapter. The writers would be compensated with royalties based on the number of their pages and the sales receipts from the books. I agreed to participate and appropriately named my chapter "I Enjoyed It!"

In 1975, Rodale Press published a two-volume set of the books. These were described as absorbing stories of forty-six men and women who had hiked the entire Appalachian Trail. Preceding my article was a three-page write-up about Earl Shaffer and his 1948 and 1965 hikes.

Shortly after these books came out, I saw Shaffer at the biennial Appalachian Trail Conference meeting. I remarked that he did not write much. He said that he did not write anything for the books. When Rodale Press contacted him about the royalties program, he told them he would send in an article, but instead of any royalty he wanted them to print one hundred copies of his book, *Walking With Spring*. Rodale Press refused his offer.

Showing Shaffer the set of books I had with me, I tried to give them to him. He refused, saying, "I don't want anything to do with them!" I told him I wanted him to read just my story. I had my fingers all set and was preparing to tear out my pages. He stopped me and said he would accept the books. I was very glad he took them. I knew he would enjoy reading about all the hikes.

In 1980, the Georgia Wilderness Society with Thom Phillips as president initiated the Gene Espy Award. The award is presented annually to the individual or individuals who are considered most outstanding in their work and environmental concern in the middle Georgia area.

CHAPTER 21

Earl Shaffer, My Friend

Hearing about Earl Shaffer from the Virginia dairy farmer piqued my interest about him. What was he like? What gave him strength to hike the rugged Appalachian Trail daily until he completed his goal? What did he do after his hike? I found some answers along the Trail as I walked it.

At a lean-to in Connecticut, I found a card left by Shaffer dated June 18, 1948. It read:

"Left Georgia April 4, 1948. Expect to reach Maine August 1 -
The flowers bloom, the songbirds sing,
And though it be sun or rain,
I walk the mountaintops with spring
From Georgia north to Maine."

In another shelter I found a second note from Shaffer with the Bible quotation from Psalms 121:

"I will lift up mine eyes unto the hills, from whence

cometh my help. My help cometh from the Lord."

I left these three-year-old notes in the shelters where I found them. They were too special to be removed.

Shaffer's 1948 accomplishment of hiking from Georgia to Maine in one continuous hike was literally unbelievable at the time. At first the Appalachian Trail Conference did not accept his having thru-hiked the Trail. Myron Avery had long considered and published articles about such a feat as being impossible. After seeing Shaffer's many photographs, signatures in various Trail registers, notes, and statements from people who saw him, Shaffer was recorded by the

ATC as the very first thru-hiker of the Appalachian Trail.

Earl Shaffer, the first thru-hiker, and I, the second thru-hiker, meet for the first time at the Appalachian Trail Conference meeting at Skyland Lodge in 1952. Our friendship continued until his death 2002.

I first met Shaffer at the Twelfth Appalachian Trail Conference at Skyland Lodge in the Shenandoah National Park in 1952. (I looked a little more presentable than on my first visit as a hiker to the same lodge the year before.) We had a big time sharing experiences. We were the only two people there who really knew the rugged, deplorable conditions of much of the Appalachian Trail.

Eugenia and I married in 1954 in Georgia and drove to Niagara Falls on our honeymoon. On our return, we stopped in York, Pennsylvania, and I introduced my bride to Shaffer. It was intriguing to observe his simple lifestyle. He and I enjoyed talking about the Appalachian Trail. He also told us about his antiques repair business, which sparked Eugenia's interest.

In the fall of 1965, Eugenia and I, along with our two daughters, Ellen and Jane, visited the North Georgia mountains to see the beautiful fall leaves. We stopped at Unicoi Gap, where Ellen, Jane, and I started hiking north on the Appalachian Trail, also known by then as "Daddy's Trail."

We had not gone beyond the sight of our car when we heard a loud sound of a creature crunching through the fall leaves as it came down the Trail. We stood still, looking up the mountain through the foliage. My little girls thought surely it was a bear and were simultaneously curious and terrified. To their great relief, it was an approaching lone hiker. I told my daughters that I could tell that the hiker had come from a long distance. They were so excited to meet a hiker actually on the Trail. I asked the hiker where he had started. When he replied it was Maine, I exclaimed, "Earl Shaffer!" He said, "Gene Espy!"

I had no idea he was on the Trail again. Only five minutes earlier or later, we wouldn't have met. We joyfully took Shaffer into Helen, Georgia, and helped him replace some of his worn clothing and depleted food supply. Shaffer said he was behind schedule to meet his brother at Springer Mountain. He also shared with us that he had about decided to quit as he was "trail weary." We took him back to the Appalachian Trail and encouraged him on to Springer Mountain. Later he told me that meeting up with us was the boost he had needed to finish his north to south thru-hike.

Meeting a real thru-hiker in action gave my wide-eyed daughters some idea of what I had experienced on the Appalachian Trail. The fact that it was the legendary Earl Shaffer himself made the encounter that much richer.

After that, Earl and I would see each other at some of the Appalachian Trail Conferences and Appalachian Long Distance Hikers Association Gatherings. In 1998, I was asked to be the replacement for Earl Shaffer as the main speaker at an ALDHA Gathering in West Virginia. He had not finished his third thru-hike in time to speak due to difficult trail conditions. We corresponded until his death on May 5, 2002, at the age of eighty-three.

Nov. 11, 1998

Dear Gene,

I was happy to hear from you. It was a long hard journey, much more difficult than when we did it long ago. More peaks and much rough and rocky trailway has replaced the traditional A.T. They even have wading of streams in Maine and have bypassed the towns and sporting camps. If my brother John had not come to Maine and supplied me with food and occasional shuttles to town I probably wouldn't have finished the trip. When various reporters asked if I would do the thru hike again my reply was to the point. "No". I was horrified at the rock climbing, bog hazards and the stream wading. Some of those rock climbs are exceedingly dangerous.

Very few of the thru hikers actually are "purist"! Most bypass some of the worst stretches. I don't blame them. I fell many times and was lucky to escape serious injury. I believe and tell people I have a guardian angel.

The meeting of ALDHA in Carlisle last year was very nice. I regret I had to miss this year for obvious reasons. Apparently Chester was there this year. He met me at a road crossing along the way and we recalled our early trips. I once met Owen Allen after his hike with a friend.

Sincerely,
Earl

Earl Shaffer wrote this letter telling me about his last thru-hike in 1998.

CHAPTER 22

More Adventures

Ready for another outdoor adventure and liking boats as well as I did, I dreamed up a long boat trip in 1953. I planned to travel down Georgia's Ocmulgee River, follow the Atlantic Intracoastal Waterway to New York City, Hudson River, Erie Canal, Lake Erie, Lake Michigan, Illinois and Mississippi Canal, Mississippi River, New Orleans, the Gulf Intracoastal Waterway, around Florida, up the Atlantic Intracoastal Waterway, and back up the Ocmulgee River to my starting point.

I anticipated using my homemade seventeen-foot outboard cruiser for this 6,000 to 7,000-mile boat trip. I secured and studied maps and other government publications. I needed a twenty-five-horsepower outboard motor, the largest being manufactured at that time.

Feeling confident, I wrote Johnson Motors about my plans and asked them to sponsor my trip. I enclosed a news clipping about my Appalachian Trail hike to let them know I had the resourcefulness and stamina to make such a boat trip. I mailed the letter and hoped.

It was thrilling when I received a reply letter from Johnson Motors agreeing to furnish me with a motor and to alert the Johnson dealers along my route. It seemed like a win-win situation for everyone.

At this time I was working for the Harris Foundry and Machine Company in Cordele, Georgia. Upon receipt of the Johnson Motors letter, I discussed my plans with my boss, the manager of the plant where I worked. I asked for a five-week leave of absence in addition to my week's vacation time already earned. He refused, saying he needed me and could not allow me to miss that much time. I valued my job, so I sighed deeply and declined the offer from Johnson Motors.

515-14 Avenue East
Cordele, Georgia
May 29, 1953

Johnson Motors
Waukegan, Illinois

Dear Sirs:

I am completing plans for about a 6000-7000 mile boat trip. I have a 17 foot outboard cruiser and am fitting it out for the trip.

I live near the Ocmulgee River about 200 miles inland. I plan to go down this river (Made this trip before), follow the Atlantic Intracoastal Waterway to New York City, Hudson River, Erie Canal, Lake Erie, Lake Huron, Lake Michigan, Illinois and Mississippi Canal, Mississippi River, New Orleans, The Gulf Intracoastal Waterway and around Florida, up the Atlantic Intracoastal Waterway, and back up the Ocmulgee River to my starting point.

This trip may sound a bit long and hard but I am confident that I will make it. The enclosed newspaper clipping describes one of my previous experiences.

I plan to start this trip the last part of June and hope to finish early in August.

I have the maps and other government publications relative to my route. I do not have a listing of Johnson Authorized Service Stations.

I am 26 years old, a graduate of Georgia Tech, and work as an engineer-draftsman. Boating has been my main hobby for about 10 years. I have made several outboards and an inboard hydroplane.

Since 1941, Lee Espy, my father, has been the Secretary-Treasurer of the Cordele Hardware Company, the Johnson dealer for this vicinity.

I am a firm believer in Johnson Motors and would like to use a 25 H.P. Johnson on my trip.

I am wondering if your company would like to take any part of sponsoring this trip. I believe I could give whatever motor I used some favorable publicity.

Sincerely yours,

Eugene M. Espy

I wrote this proposal to Johnson Motors requesting them to sponsor me on a 6000-7000 boat trip.

Johnson

JOHNSON MOTORS, WAUKEGAN, ILLINOIS, U.S.A.

DIVISION OF OUTBOARD, MARINE & MANUFACTURING COMPANY

June 3, 1953

Mr. Eugene M. Espy
515 Fourteenth Avenue, East
Cordele, Georgia

Dear Mr. Espy:

Thank you for your interesting letter of May 29, and your interest in Johnson. Your trip sounds interesting, and should prove to be quite an experience.

Regarding the sponsership of your trip, about the best we can do is furnish you a 25 to make the trip with. Company policy forbids us from making any other type of agreement with individuals wishing to make such trips as you contemplate. Since we receive numerous requests such as yours, you can understand why we even have to restrict the number of motors we consign for such purposes.

However, we will furnish you with a motor for your use, and will try to alert Johnson dealers, along your route, to help you in any way they can.

Should this proposal interest you, please send us a detailed itinerary of your proposed trip, giving approximate dates of arrival at ports you plan to stop in. With this information, we may be of some publicity assistance.

Thanks again for writing us.

Cordially,

E. L. (Buck) Rogers
Asst. Publicity Manager

ELR/js

The ONLY manufacturer who has built A MILLION OUTBOARD MOTORS

Johnson Motors agreed in this letter to sponsor me on my long boat trip.

* * *

About two years after I completed my Appalachian Trail thru-hike, I built a seventeen-foot boat for use with a 25-horsepower outboard motor. A cabin enclosed the front. In July 1953, I traveled in this homemade boat on a 300-mile solo trip down the Ocmulgee River to Daytona Beach. Without having to walk and carry a backpack, I enjoyed racing down the river. On the curves I was careful to steer to avoid sand build-up on the inside and on the outside dodge trees that had fallen into the river when they were undermined by the current. While cruising down the river, I enjoyed drinking Royal Crown Colas and eating Moon Pies.

At Darien I went south on the Intracoastal Waterway past Brunswick to Daytona Beach. While crossing the mouth of the Saint John's River at Jacksonville, I noticed some military fighter planes flying around in the distance. Suddenly, as I was seated in the forward cabin using remote controls, I heard and felt a tremendous roar and vibration. It really scared me. I thought it must be a serious motor problem, so I quickly shut it off and figured out the source of the noise. A military plane had dived behind me and had flown just a few feet above me. I hoped they at least had fun.

I went on to Daytona Beach and docked my boat. I hitchhiked back to Cordele, picked up my father's car with my boat trailer attached, and drove to Daytona Beach. I floated my boat onto the trailer and brought it home from its two-day river cruise. The *Cordele Dispatch* newspaper published an article about my latest adventure.

* * *

In 1953, Eugenia had graduated from college and was in her first year of teaching in Tifton, forty miles south of Cordele. One weekend night I decided to drive to Tifton in my '37 Ford car for a

Espy Completes 300 Mile Solo In 17-Ft. Boat

By JACK AESCHLIMAN
Dispatch Staff Writer

Richard Halliburton, f a m e d world traveler, had little on a 26-year-old Cordelean when it comes to unusual travels.

Gene Espy, Cordele's young adventurer who took a 2,050 mile hike on a mountain path in 1951, has done it again, This time, however, he decided not to take it out on shoe leather

and he went on a solo boat trip.

Traveling 300 miles down the Okmulgee River from Abbeville, to St. Simon's Island, thence to Jacksonville, Ga., and to St. Augustine, Fla., Gene made the trip by himself, with no one to talk to or look at for two days.

He slept on the boat—a 17 foot cruiser with a 25 horsepower outboard motor —overnight. When asked why he decided to make this unusual excursion by himself, he replied "I like to fool around with boats and decided to take this as my vacation."

Gene's the boy who made Life Magazine as a result of his hike along a mountain path from Mt. Oglethorpe, Ga., to Mt. Katadin, Me. This 2,050 mile hike is the longest mountain path in the world, Gene said.

It took him from May to Ceptember to complete the trek, but he'd had the gratifying experience that few people, if any, had ever done what he'd just finished doing.

Like Richrd Halliburton, who was last heard from riding in a Chinese junk headed across the Pacific toward the United States, this Gene Espy has the blood of an adventurer in his veins.

It's this blood that keeps life from being just an everybody drudge and Cordele should be thankful for having a guy such as Gene to keep on the outlook for some new adventure to tackle. You get to feeling like a traveler yourself just talking to him.

Inside my homemade seventeen-foot boat, I am readying for launch in the Ocmulgee River.

A friend took this photo from a bridge as I cruised down the Ocmulgee River at the beginning of my 300 mile solo boat trip to Daytona Beach.

date with Eugenia. She rode in the car to the nice Alpine Restaurant, but did not want to be seen riding in such an old, beat-up car. She was thankful for the rain and darkness that night. Still, Eugenia was very concerned. If the parents of her students were to see her, what would they think? Tifton was a small town, and teachers were to set a good example. Frankly, it was funny to me. I was definitely in love with Eugenia, however, so I never went to see her in that particular car again. After our marriage in July 1954, we traveled on our long honeymoon in a brand new gold and white (Georgia Tech colors) Plymouth car.

* * *

I was back on the Appalachian Trail for a few days in 1953, when I met Fred A. Birchmore and his wife, Willa Deane, on the Trail in Georgia. Living in Athens, Georgia, they were leading a group of Girl Scouts on a day hike. Our mutual love of adventure connected us immediately and formed the basis for our friendship that carries on today. Fred has had many, many spectacular worldwide adventures. In 1935-36 he bicycled around the world! He described this in *Around the World on a Bicycle*, the first book to be printed by the University of Georgia Press at Athens, Georgia. Fred and his All-American tennis champion son, Danny, thru-hiked the Appalachian Trail in 1975.

By 1958, Mount Oglethorpe had lost some of its wilderness appearance due to the half dozen chicken houses within sight. The Appalachian Trail Conference and the Georgia Appalachian Trail Club abandoned the first twenty miles of the Trail, thus moving the southern Trail terminus northward to Springer Mountain in the Chattahoochee National Forest. Springer Mountain is usually reached from Amicalola Falls State Park, located nineteen miles west of Dahlonega, Georgia. The northern end remains the mile-high Mount Katahdin, the highest mountain in Maine. Today the revised

Trail is about 2,175 miles long.

In March 1981, Fred, Ed Selby, Darrell Maret, and I hiked the twenty miles of abandoned Trail from Mount Oglethorpe through Amicalola Falls State Park to Springer Mountain, the revised terminus of the Appalachian Trail. Each of us had previously hiked the entire Appalachian Trail, but I was the only one who had started at Mount Oglethorpe. We wanted to see what that part of the Trail would look like in these later years before any development encroached farther.

On the road to Mount Oglethorpe a locked gate blocked our path. Though there was also a "No Trespassing" sign, we left our car at the gate and walked to the top of Mount Oglethorpe. There beside the communication towers we found a sadly abused statue of James Oglethorpe, founder of Georgia. As we walked along a dirt ridge road, we saw the remains of an old house and a rundown outbuilding. We could barely see the faint blazes to direct us off the ridge road.

While hiking the paved road nearby, we came to some water like a spring. It was near a golf course as described in the old guidebook. We had a good view of mountains in the distance. The paved road soon became dirt, and we saw an area being prepared for development. At this point there are several forest roads. To abate our confusion, Ed took out his map and compass so we could find the direction to Highway 52. Then we hiked a dirt road between two fields until we got to a large stream. After wading across, we stopped for overnight camp along the tributary going up on the Amicalola ridge.

Our interesting conversations at supper included a comparison of our styles of backpacking. I was using the backpack I had taken on my thru-hike in 1951. It was still good enough for me thirty years later, sturdy and a little nostalgia-inducing.

As we got up the next morning it was raining. The pattering sound of the raindrops pelting the leaves brought back memories. A little later the rain stopped and it turned colder. The woods smelled so fresh and earthy. Then to our surprise it started snowing! What an unexpected treat! I had never experienced snow falling in the wilderness. The branches of the trees accentuated in their white frosting of snow made for a beautiful sight. Hiking with some snow crunching beneath my feet was quite different.

We stayed on the old Trail and other back roads, eventually reaching a well-traveled road within a developed road. We continued following the ridge into Amicalola Falls State Park as the Trail pairs with the road going behind the cabins at the top of the falls. We proceeded on the blue blaze Approach Trail down to the ranger station at the base of the falls.

At the top of Springer Mountain, we found one of the several identical plaques for identifying the Trail for which Warner W. Hall, president of the GATC posed in 1934. The plaque at Springer reads:

> APPALACHIAN TRAIL GEORGIA TO MAINE
> A FOOTPATH FOR THOSE
> WHO SEEK FELLOWSHIP
> WITH THE WILDERNESS
> THE GEORGIA APPALACHIAN TRAIL CLUB, 1934

We all enjoyed the memorable hike together, but it made us sad to see the ruins of the pre-1958 Trail. The old Trail route has been transgressed by development and its environment is less than a wilderness. The statue of James Oglethorpe has since been reconditioned and is currently on display in Jasper, Georgia.

* * *

In 1991, the United States Forest Service, in cooperation with the Appalachian Trail Conference, erected a large sign depicting the Appalachian Trail at Hog Pen Gap, Georgia. The Plexiglas and steel

I pose in 1983 carrying my backpack in front of the oil painting, by a Maine artist, depicting my completed thru-hike at the foot of Mount Katahdin.

sign was situated by the Trail where it crosses the Richard B. Russell Scenic Parkway. No road existed here in 1951.

A brief history about the origin of the Appalachian Trail and picture of Benton MacKaye are shown. Also featured are a map of the Trail and various photographs. The sign also shows a 1951 picture of a hiking Gene Espy. The following 1951 editorial from the Lewiston, Maine *Daily Sun* is shown. *"In the space of 123 days Gene Espy walked 2,025 miles, wore out 3 pairs of shoes, killed 15 rattlesnakes with his walking stick, grew a long beard, and lost 28 pounds. He was the second man in history to cover the full length of the Trail, which winds from Mt. Oglethorpe northward over hundreds of other summits to central Maine, in one continuous effort. To those acquainted with the Trail, it is a feat of endurance that stamps the young Georgian as a man of fortitude and courage."*

This was quite an honor for me to be included in this sign. The sign stayed in place several years, but repeated vandalism became its downfall.

* * *

My years of being in the working world ended in 1995 with my retirement from my job as an aerospace engineer at Robins Air Force Base, Georgia. My wanderlust promptly popped up again as I found more time to relax and enjoy the outdoors. Reflecting on my youthful endeavors, I decided I wanted to experience the Trail conditions in Georgia.

My always supportive wife drove me in 1995 to Deep Gap, North Carolina, in the Nantahala National Forest. I hiked alone south through the seventy-six-mile Georgia section to Springer Mountain. It was the middle of April, so I met a lot of would-be thru-hikers headed north. I enjoyed the experience immensely, talking to and encouraging those who wanted to stop for a minute or so. During

I pose in 1991 beside the section of the Appalachian Trail sign honoring me at Hogpen Gap, Georgia, where the Trail crosses the Richard B. Russell Scenic Parkway.

Turner Broadcasting Systems filmed me in 2003 for the Appalachian Trail segment in its Turner South television program. Here I am standing on the Approach Trail to Springer Mountain.

my weeklong hike, I met seven dogs hiking with their masters. Most hikers are careful with their dogs, but I surprisingly used my staff to flip dog poop from the middle of the Trail several times. I'd rather have dog poop to deal with than a snake, though.

Much lighter – that's how I would describe the "new-fangled" equipment that I carried on my 1995 hike. I enjoyed researching and purchasing the new equipment. It was so much easier to be able to make buying decisions in a store for specially designed hiking equipment than my early days of scrounging through catalogs and guessing. Along with my new tent, backpack, hiking shoes, flashlight, and water bottle, I also brought along some things from my 1951 hike. I used the same cook stove, collapsible cup, snakebite kit, cooking pans, and utensils. Lightweight food and candy bars were my staples. One main difference was the addition of the water purification equipment now necessary.

I left my revered 1951 hiking staff in its place of honor in my home. Instead, I carried Eugenia's hiking stick. Made of hickory, the stick had been cut by a friend and given to her for use on her daily walks. It worked just fine for my hike.

I experienced in 1951 an Appalachian Trail in Georgia so overgrown that I had to bushwhack parts of it. During my 1995 hike, I found the Trail to be in superb condition and easy to follow. I could find a place to pitch my tent every night that week.

The Georgia Appalachian Trail Club does a fine job of maintaining the Trail in Georgia. Each mile is assigned to a member responsible for maintenance. From what I have heard, the GATC has currently the best reputation of all the maintaining clubs of the Trail. I did not know of the GATC before my 1951 thru-hike. Upon returning to Georgia, I was told they voted unanimously to waiver all existing membership requirements and accept me. I felt truly honored. I've been a member ever since.

* * *

Over ten years ago, one of my friends called the L.L. Bean Company in Freeport, Maine, about a purchase. When she and the salesman proceeded to talk about the Appalachian Trail, my friend informed him she lived in the same neighborhood as the second thru-hiker. He immediately asked if she lived close to Gene Espy. My friend was surprised at his knowledge.

On their website in 2004, L.L. Bean featured me blazing the Appalachian Trail as the second thru-hiker. The text mentioned that I still have the L.L. Bean Maine Guide shoes that I used on the Trail after purchasing them in 1951 for $9.95. The fact that the rugged, rocky Appalachian Trail attracted few hikers at that time was compared with the well-traveled Trail presently enjoyed by thousands of hikers today.

Amazingly, my 1951 thru-hike continues to interest people even in recent years. Newspaper articles about my thru-hike are still written. The *Georgia Tech Alumni Magazine* featured my thru-hike as the cover story in its Fall 2005 edition. I have been featured in television programs by Turner South and Georgia Public Broadcasting's "Georgia On My Mind." I often give presentations to groups, large or small. I never tire of talking about my thru-hike and encouraging conservation of the Appalachian Trail and other wilderness areas.

My wife Eugenia and I.

* * *

Eugenia and I are thrilled that our daughters, Ellen and Jane, have passed down the love of the outdoors to their daughters, Courtney and Amanda. Courtney has done extensive hiking, reaching the peaks of over half of the highest mountains in the Adirondacks. She dreams of following in the footsteps of her grandfather as a thru-hiker on the Appalachian Trail. Although Amanda is much younger, she savors any time she can get in the mountains and enjoys hiking with the family.

The intense determination that enabled me to successfully complete such an exceptional feat has repeatedly inspired me and each member of my family to persevere through life's many challenges. My children and grandchildren tell me they have gained strength through my experiences.

My entire family seems to never tire of hearing my adventure stories. Our favorite storytelling times take place in the mountains under the glimmering stars on a clear, peaceful night.

In 2005 I was walking at Amicalola Falls State Park, Georgia. Photo by Gary W. Meek.